ANIMAL WELFARE

Dedication

To those in the front line

ANIMAL
WELFARE

COLIN SPEDDING

Earthscan Publications Ltd, London and Sterling, VA

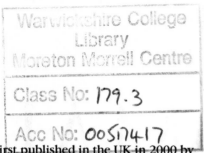
First published in the UK in 2000 by
Earthscan Publications Ltd

Copyright © Colin Spedding, 2000

A catalogue record for this book is available from the British Library

ISBN: 1 85383 672 9 paperback
       1 85383 671 0 hardback

Typesetting by JS Typesetting, Wellingborough, Northants
Printed and bound by Creative Print and Design, Wales
Cover design by Susanne Harris

For a full list of publications please contact:

Earthscan Publications Ltd
120 Pentonville Road
London, N1 9JN, UK
Tel: +44 (0)20 7278 0433
Fax: +44 (0)20 7278 1142
Email: earthinfo@earthscan.co.uk
http://www.earthscan.co.uk

22883 Quicksilver Drive, Sterling, VA 20166–2012, USA

Earthscan is an editorially independent subsidiary of Kogan Page
Ltd and publishes in association with WWF-UK and the International
Institute for Environment and Development

This book is printed on elemental chlorine-free paper

Contents

Contents

List of Tables

List of Boxes

Preface

Reviewing the suffering of animals in the world can be a depressing experience, but reviewing the efforts made by all those working in the front line, to reduce suffering, eradicate cruelty, to rescue, treat and rehabilitate animals, is both impressive and encouraging. I hope this book will help them by increasing public awareness of both the problems and their efforts to solve them.

In talking to many different groups about animal welfare, it became very clear that people who were closely involved with animals generally got used to what they were doing but that this often looked very different to those not so involved. And this was true independent of whether the animals were farm livestock, laboratory animals, show animals, pets or animals used for sport or entertainment.

Those involved generally believe that they are caring for their animals, but often with little knowledge of their welfare needs and how they should be kept.

Much poor welfare – and even cruelty – is caused by ignorance or simply thoughtlessness: so awareness needs encouragement.

All this led me to the view that, whatever one's own involvement, it is helpful to think about the welfare of other animals, kept for other purposes by other people.

I have written this book in the hope that a wider view will help to clarify our own responsibilities as animal keepers and as citizens, and result in greater support for those in the front line.

Acknowledgements

I am greatly indebted to the many animal welfare organizations for the unstinting help that they have provided in the preparation of this book.

Nearly all the organizations listed in Table 6.3 and in Appendix 2 have gone to a great deal of trouble to send me information, not only about their aims, objectives and activities but their views on what are the major issues now and for the future. I had to resist the temptation to describe all their impressive work in detail: this was not feasible, but it deserves to be better known and I hope that the organizations will receive ever-increasing support from the public.

I am also greatly indebted to my secretary, Mrs Mary Jones, for all her help at all stages of writing and seeing the book through to completion.

Acronyms and Abbreviations

AHA	American Humane Association
AHT	Animal Health Trust
AI	Artificial insemination
ACT	Animal Care Trust
ANZCCART	Australia and New Zealand Council for the Care of Animals in Research and Teaching
APC	Animal Procedures Committee
ASPCA	American Society for the Prevention of Cruelty to Animals
AWA	Animal Welfare Act (USA)
AWAC	Animal Welfare Advisory Committee (New Zealand)
BDH	Battersea Dogs Home
BFF	Born Free Foundation
BSE	Bovine spongiform encephalopathy
BST	Bovine somatotrophin
BVA	British Veterinary Association
CAP	Common Agricultural Policy
CAWC	Companion Animal Welfare Council
CFHS	Canadian Federation of Humane Societies
CITES	Convention on International Trade in Endangered Species
CIWF	Compassion in World Farming
CT	Computed Tomography
DNA	Deoxyribonucleic acid
DSPA	Dutch Society for the Protection of Animals
EC	European Commission
EEC	European Economic Community
EHPPS	Essex Horse and Pony Protection Society

ET	Embryo Transfer
EU	European Union
FASS	Federation of Animal Science Societies
FAWAC	Farm Animal Welfare Advisory Committee
FAWC	Farm Animal Welfare Council
FCE	Food Conversion Efficiency
FDR	Federal Democratic Republic (Germany)
FRAME	Fund for the Replacement of Animals in Medical Experiments
GATT	General Agreement on Tariffs and Trade
HRT	Hormone Replacement Therapy
HSA	Humane Slaughter Association
HSUS	Humane Society of the United States
IFAW	International Fund for Animal Welfare
ISO	International Organization for Standardization Committee
IUCN	International Union for the Conservation of Nature
IUDZG	International Union of Directors of Zoological Gardens
LD_{50}	Lethal Dose 50
MAFF	Ministry of Agriculture, Fisheries and Food
MRI	Magnetic Resonance Imaging
MSPCA	Massachusetts Society for the Prevention of Cruelty to Animals
NAEAC	National Animal Ethics Advisory Committee (New Zealand)
NCDL	National Canine Defence League
NVBD	Ned Ver tot Bescherming van Dieren
PDSA	People's Dispensary for Sick Animals
PMS	Pregnant Mare Serum
PMU	Pregnant Mare Urine
RCD	Rabbit Calcivirus Disease
RDS	Research Defence Society
RNZSPCA	Royal New Zealand Society for the Prevention of Cruelty to Animals
RSPCA	Royal Society for the Prevention of Cruelty to Animals
RVC ACT	Royal Veterinary College Animal Care Trust
SPANA	Society for the Protection of Animals Abroad
SSC	Captive Breeding Specialist Group of IUCN

SSPCA	Scottish Society for the Prevention of Cruelty to Animals
STS	Schweizer Tierschutz
TB	Tuberculosis
UFAW	Universities Federation for Animal Welfare
UKEG	UK Elephant Group
UKXIRA	United Kingdom Xenotransplantation Interim Regulatory Authority
USAMRICD	United States Army Medical Research Institute of Chemical Defense
WAN	World Animal Net
WSPA	World Society for the Protection of Animals
WTO	World Trade Organization
WZCS	World Zoo Conservation Strategy

Glossary

Arachnids Spiders and related animals, characterized by possessing eight legs

Bovine somatotrophin (BST) A hormone injected into cows to increase milk output

Cellulase An enzyme for digesting cellulose not normally possessed by animals

Cetaceans Members of the whale and dolphin family

Chelonians An order including tortoises, turtles and terrapins

Cloning Duplicating animals or plants without sexual reproduction

Conspecifics Other animals of the same species

Coprophagia Eating one's own faeces (called 'refection' in rabbits)

Declawing Removal of claws (in birds, dew and pivot claws)

Displasia Displacement of the hip

Draize Test Standard test for ophthalmic irritancy

Dubbing Removal of all or part of the male comb (in poultry)

Embryo transfer (ET) The transfer of an embryo from one female animal to another – whether of the same species or not

Hinny Cross between a male horse and a female donkey

In vitro Outside the live animal

In vivo In the live animal

LD_{50} The dose level of a substance that kills 50 per cent of the animals dosed

Monoclonal antibody An antibody produced artificially from a cell clone and therefore consisting of a single type of immunoglobulin

Mule A cross between a male donkey and a female horse

Mules operation An operation, used in Australia, to reduce skin folds above the tail in Merino sheep

Mutilations Defined as procedures carried out for other than therapeutic or diagnostic purposes and resulting in damage to or the loss of a sensitive part of the body or the alteration of bone structure, or causing a significant amount of pain and distress

Pelagic Relating to the open sea

Pharming The keeping of animals for the production of pharmaceuticals

Pheromones Chemicals given off by animals, usually to attract a mate; often effective at great distances

Raptor Bird of prey

Sentience Capacity to suffer

'Spent' hens Laying hens that have finished their productive lives

Stereotypies Prolonged, obsessive performance of apparently purposeless activity

Surrogate mothers Substitute mothers, bearing the offspring of others

Transgenic animal An animal into which new DNA sequences have been deliberately introduced

Vegetarians Those who eat no meat but may consume eggs and dairy products

Vegans Those who eat no animal products at all

Xenotransplantation The transplantation of tissues or organs from one species into an individual of another species

Zoochosis Mental damage due to captivity

1

Introduction

'Our civilization is largely defined by the way living beings are respected and how we deal with them'
(van Wifen)

An important starting point is how we define animal welfare (see Chapter 2). Clearly, it is difficult to make any progress – even in discussion – if we all mean different things by the same words. Simply bandying about highly-individual opinions on welfare is hardly likely to be productive.

It would be a laudable objective for society to have an agreed definition, but that would not prevent individuals disagreeing with it and trying to persuade others of their point of view.

Even so, an agreed definition – or one accepted by society – acts as a focus for debate and a form of words that can be the target for improvement. After all, attitudes to animals, their welfare and the importance of fostering it, have all changed over time and still vary greatly from one country and region to another.

In the UK, for example, attitudes to bear-baiting, cock-fighting, dog-fighting and badger-baiting have changed markedly over the years, as have views on the ways in which working horses, pets and farm animals should be treated.

Currently, the debate focuses on the hunting of wild animals, the culling of over-numerous populations, the control of pests and the ways in which animals are kept on farms and in zoos and circuses, but the emphasis is quite different in different countries.

Chapter 3 discusses the question of which animals should be included in our concerns for welfare, in our own and in other countries. For, as with the treatment of people, concern cannot simply be confined to one's own village, town or nation. It is wise to be clear about exactly *why* we should be concerned anyway (see Chapter 2) and the extent to which this should be related to the nature and scale of the problem (see Chapter 4). For example, there are more chickens than cows, more wildlife (of some species) killed on the roads than in hunting, more marine fish killed than freshwater fish and so on. Does this affect how concerned we should be?

In any case, we have to ask what 'the problem' is. Just because a lot of animals are involved, does it follow that there *is* a problem? Or is it that, if there is a problem, it is a bigger or more important one if large numbers are involved?

In all this – and this will be a recurring theme – to an animal that is suffering, it does not make any difference whether it is the only one or one of thousands; just as it does not matter to the animal *why* anything is being done to it, or for what purpose. What matters to the animal is the degree, extent and duration of the suffering. So the essential questions to be asked are: Is the animal suffering? Are we sure? How can we tell? Are there signs or tests that can be used and is it the same for different species?

In some important respects, things must be different for different species. For example, if a hen suffers because it is deprived of a nest box in which to lay its eggs, this cannot be true of a bullock or a ewe. In other words, to the extent that being deprived of the opportunity to exercise natural behavioural patterns is a cause of suffering or poor welfare, it is likely that there are differences not only between species, but also between sexes, sizes and ages of a single species.

It is therefore necessary to lay down standards for the ways that different animals are kept, in general terms but also, it turns out, in very great detail. The need for such standards is discussed in Chapter 5. This requires a great deal of information, from scientific investigation and from practical experience, because standards have to be based on evidence. Some people will argue that it is perfectly obvious when an animal is suffering and, in some cases, this is obviously true. Not always, however. For instance, grazing animals, such as cattle and sheep, have evolved not to show pain, in order not to reveal weakness to a watching predator. Television regularly illustrates spectacular examples of antelope leaping about in an exaggerated manner as if to say to a predator 'don't bother with me, I'm exceptionally fit and therefore difficult to catch'. So it does not follow that because we observe no sign of pain that the animal is not suffering. Humans also vary in the degree of pain they can tolerate and the extent to which they show it.

It is customary, at this point, to warn against anthropomorphism, believing that, because we would be distressed by something, therefore the animal must be similarly affected. Clearly, we cannot assume that because we would feel pain from something, the animal does so too. We cannot know that it does; but, equally, we cannot know that it does not! We should therefore keep an open mind and base our judgement on evidence wherever possible.

Unfortunately, evidence may be lacking and very hard to obtain. In many cases, one would not wish to see the necessary experiments carried out to produce hard evidence. Fortunately, the technology of painlessly assessing all kinds of changes in the physiology and behaviour of unconstrained animals is developing very rapidly.

In many cases, we only need the evidence of our eyes: a goat dropped from a tower requires no supporting evidence (much less experimental evidence) to tell us that intolerable suffering is involved. Even in this obvious example, it is salutary to ask how we actually know that the animal suffers. This is not to suggest that it does not, but it may be helpful, in judging rather less obvious cases, to be clear about our reasoning. Bear in mind that dropping from a great height is not a problem for very small animals, such as ducklings of tree-nesting ducks and mice. In the first example, this is what happens in nature – ducklings simply drop to the ground and run off. The fact is that the smaller the animal, the greater its surface area relative to its weight, and this greatly affects its air resistance. If *we* wish to descend safely, we increase our air resistance by means of a parachute.

Where there is real doubt about whether an animal suffers, it is preferable to give the animal the benefit of it and assume that a practice should be avoided if there is a possibility that it causes unacceptable suffering. It is necessary to insert words like unacceptable, however suspect they may appear, because suffering is a part of life. Giving birth may involve considerable suffering, so may some fighting between animals that is necessary to establish a hierarchy of dominance, whether in a herd of dairy cows or between competing stags.

Where wild animals are concerned, we cannot sensibly interfere in their lives: predators must live as well as prey. But if we do interfere, we acquire responsibilities for welfare. If we exhibit dolphins in a pool, we have interfered, often in ways that we do not understand or even know about. This is also an example where most of us would need no evidence to support our instinct that, for example, too small a pool is being used. Where it is right that standards should be set, how can they be enforced? Who is going to act? Who is already doing what about it? These are the questions posed in Chapter 6.

Since there is much that needs to be done, Chapters 7 and 8 discuss how improvements in animal welfare can be best achieved – and by whom. Many people are not sure what they could do or, indeed, what needs to be done, but, in any case, feel that they can make very little difference by themselves. This is by no means always true: all those who consume animal products could refuse to buy those that have involved cruelty or poor welfare, and those who pay to go to animal circuses or watch dancing bears, for example, could stop doing so.

Fortunately, individuals do not have to act entirely on their own. There are at least 6000 animal welfare organizations across the world, in total doing an enormous amount of good in an astonishing number of ways. Some rehouse stray dogs and cats, some rescue wild animals from natural disaster and war zones, some deal with the casualties of pollution (eg oiled sea-birds), some lobby governments to bring about changes in the law (all dealt with in Chapter 6). All welcome members and need supporters, in however small a way.

So there are many ways in which we can all help, including persuading others that we all have responsibilities, as citizens. By a citizen I simply mean one who belongs to a human society (eg a town, city, state, nation or organized group of nations) in the sense that one has accepted the responsibilities and been granted the rights normally accorded by that society to its citizens. In other words, citizenship has to be conferred on an individual and can be withdrawn if the rules of that society are seriously infringed. Both rights and responsibilities may be related to age, sex, status, wealth and, historically, a whole range of other conditions.

In broad terms, the nature of the rights and responsibilities usually has certain characteristics (see Table 1.1).

Table 1.1 *Characteristic Rights and Responsibilities
of a Citizen*

Rights	Responsibilities
To play some part in the legislative proceedings of the state to which the citizen belongs	To contribute to the debates on which decisions and actions of the state are based
Freedom of speech, movement, religion, association etc, within the law	To obey the law and to exercise freedoms within it
To seek changes in the law (by appropriate means)	To avoid infringing the rights and freedoms of others
	To influence the behaviour of society in relation to its treatment of people, animals and the environment

Thus it is both the right and the responsibility of a citizen to help shape the way in which society behaves, and this includes its treatment of animals.

These responsibilities relating to animal welfare are not difficult to define in general terms (see Table 1.2) but are very hard to translate into detailed propositions, and it is the purpose of subsequent chapters to explore the problems and difficulties as well as possible solutions. Animal welfare is a subject on which many people feel very strongly and about which people may hold very different views.

However, although individuals are quite entitled to highly emotional attitudes to the ways in which animals are treated and a society in which no one cared would be intolerable to most of us, we do have to accept that such societies may exist and others also believe that they are right.

Table 1.2 *Responsibilities of the Citizen Relating to
Animal Welfare*

1 To obey the law
2 To operate personally to high standards
3 To persuade others that standards should be raised (it is unlikely that improvement will *not* be needed on any foreseeable time-scale)
4 To encourage and participate in informed debate (both public and private)
5 To acquire (and help others to acquire) the knowledge and expertise needed to discharge these responsibilities

But if every citizen has a responsibility as an individual, how can this be discharged? Is the current scene satisfactory? Are there enough well-supported organizations in the field? Is there actually a need for further action? If so, exactly what further action is needed? But the future may hold new welfare problems and, in some cases, it may be possible to avoid them by controlling the developments that cause them. Chapter 9 discusses what these developments are likely to be.

Finally, in Chapter 10, I have summarized conclusions I have reached whilst preparing this book that I did not necessarily start with, but which have confirmed my instinct that the welfare of all the different kinds of animals should be treated as one subject. Some conclusions, however, can be reached very quickly. The moral basis for concern and the principles of animal welfare should be the same for all countries and all people, but they may not be equally accepted, recognized or acted upon. Indeed, what is possible will vary from one country to another and so will the nature and scale of the problems (Chapter 4) and what is being done about them. Of course, wealthier countries can, and do, help to deal with animal welfare problems occurring outside their own boundaries, but this has to be done sensitively. In less affluent societies, improvement in animal welfare may not be economically possible. We have to recognize, for example, that those who train and exhibit dancing bears may have no other means of supporting their families.

The principles may be the same but the examples that exemplify them are different. In selecting examples to illustrate points being made, there are risks of being too parochial and giving an unbalanced picture of the current state of affairs. Even if the information was available, it would not be feasible to compile a comprehensive account of the state of animal welfare worldwide. Nor would it serve a very useful purpose, since it is far better for each country to assess its own situation.

But it has worried me considerably that, in giving examples, an unbalanced or biased picture may emerge, as if some countries (or industries) are worse or better than others. Not only would it be impossible to make such judgements, it would also be unfair: some countries are better or worse in some respects than others. So, within my own limited knowledge, but also drawing on the experience of others, I have used examples to illustrate problems and principles in the hope that it may be sufficient to warn against jumping to unjustified conclusions because of my selection.

When it comes to taking action, it is necessary to define the problem and then to identify workable, effective solutions. The people who feel most strongly, and vigorously draw attention to the fact that there is a problem, may not always be the best qualified to define exactly what it is. They may be even less able to work out effective solutions. A strong and clear moral position is needed to stand up and say 'that is a problem and it is not acceptable'. Knowledge is needed to define exactly what the problem is, and both knowledge and great clarity of thought are needed to identify effective solutions.

The purpose of the book is not to tell you what to think or what to do. It is to help you to decide both of these for yourself, by providing the necessary information and by helping you to think clearly about these issues.

To engage in a campaign to improve welfare in the future, it is necessary to have some faith that it is possible, some hope that others will share your aims, but above all clarity of thought. Faith, hope and clarity – and the greatest of these is clarity.

Summary

1   The main issue in animal welfare is to avoid inflicting suffering and, where it cannot be wholly avoided, to minimize it.
2   Citizens have both rights and responsibilities, including a concern for the welfare of animals affected by them and the society to which they belong.

2

What is Animal Welfare and Why Does it Matter?

'I have yet to encounter any problem, however complicated, which, when looked at in the proper way, did not become still more complicated'
(Poul Anderson)

Welfare is normally defined as a state of well-being, in which at least basic needs are met and suffering is minimized. It is one of those terms, sometimes called 'umbrella' words, which although we all know roughly what it means covers a multitude of different interpretations when it comes to detail. Beauty, truth and freedom are other common examples. We use such words all the time, but we know perfectly well that we shall rarely all agree about what is beautiful or true, in particular cases. Clearly what is beautiful to one may not be so to another and, being subjective, a statement about what is beautiful may actually be true for one person and not for another.

Similarly for welfare. Some people would find some things essential for their welfare which others may not, and they often appear to be related to what they are used to. But obviously this cannot be very satisfactory. Thus, being drunk or drugged may generate a feeling of well-being in some, whilst others feel entirely at home mud-wrestling, being violent to others (or even themselves), eating too much or fasting. It may even be that states of physical, mental, psychological or spiritual well-being cannot all be achieved simultaneously. That is one reason why it may be better to talk of

meeting basic needs, since they are less subject to personal preferences, habits or ambitions.

   Similar considerations apply to animals. Is it any better welfare
for an overfat dog to eat toffees than for an obese child with bad
teeth to do so? And it is no use asking the dog or child! So it
is necessary to have some objectively-set standards for personal
guidance and for the guidance of those who have responsibility for
others (see Chapter 5). 'Moderation in all things' is not a bad guide
for the areas beyond basic needs, where personal choice and discre-
tion are the only ways of meeting the special needs (or wishes) of
individuals.

   What, then, are the basic needs of animals? Some such as adequate food are positive and others such as not being physically
assaulted are negative. Box 2.1 is based on this simple division. The
resulting criteria are similar to the 'Five Freedoms' developed by
the Farm Animal Welfare Council (FAWC) for farm animals (see
Tables 2.1 and 2.2). However, there seems to be no reason why the
same criteria should not apply to other animals, such as pets, although
the purpose for which animals are kept does have a major bearing
on the ways they are kept and, for that matter, killed.

Box 2.1 *Basic Needs of Animals*

Positive
Adequate and accessible supplies of suitable food (ie satisfying nutritional and health needs in a digestible and appetizing form, appropriate
to the teeth, jaws, beaks and alimentary tract of the animal concerned).
Adequate supplies of clean, fresh water at a suitable temperature, for
drinking and bathing (where necessary).
Suitable conditions relating to the atmosphere (eg temperature, humidity,
wind/draughts, gaseous concentrations and light[1]) and underlying
surface (eg ground conditions, bedding, perching area). This may imply
housing or shelter.
Adequate space and a sufficiently stimulating environment, allowing
and encouraging the expression of those natural behavioural patterns
that are characteristic of the animal concerned and in some way
necessary for a healthy life.

Appropriate contact with other animals.

Negative
Freedom from fear and stress, over and above that which is part of normal life for the species.
Freedom from physical abuse, mutilation and avoidable pain.
Freedom from disease and injury.
Protection from predators and parasites.
Protection from damaging conditions (eg excessive exposure to solar radiation).

---

1 Light is rather different from the other parameters but is extremely important. Animals vary greatly in their requirements, which may be quite complex, involving light quality (wavelength, natural, eg sunlight, composition), quantity (light intensity), daylength (patterns of light/dark) and variation in space (so that animals can seek what they want at different times). Some animals prefer to live in the dark (it follows that there is no satisfactory way in which such animals can be exhibited, for example).

Table 2.1 *The Five Freedoms*

1	*Freedom from hunger and thirst*	by ready access to fresh water and a diet to maintain full health and vigour.
2	*Freedom from discomfort*	by providing an appropriate environment including shelter and a comfortable resting area.
3	*Freedom from pain, injury or disease*	by prevention or rapid diagnosis and treatment.
4	*Freedom to express normal behaviour*	by providing sufficient space, proper facilities and company of the animal's own kind.
5	*Freedom from fear and distress*	by ensuring conditions and treatment which avoid mental suffering.

Table 2.2 *In Response to the Five Freedoms*

In response to the Five Freedoms, FAWC argues that those who have care of livestock should practise:

1 caring and responsible planning and management;
2 skilled, knowledgeable and conscientious stockmanship;
3 appropriate environmental design (eg of the husbandry system);
4 considerate handling and transport;
5 humane slaughter.

Since no animal lives forever and death is inevitable, the end of life does have to be considered for all animals kept by us; it may not be our concern for wild animals. Many farm animals are slaughtered at an earlier age than would occur in equivalent non-farm species but it is also the case that most wild animals die or are killed at ages well below their potential life span. If they do not die early, they may suffer greatly from disease, injury, exposure to bad weather, parasites or starvation. 'Natural' death is not generally very pleasant (see Box 2.2 for a discussion of the term 'natural').

Clearly, if killing the animal is our decision, good welfare has to mean a painless death – it can hardly be without injury and can hardly be thought about in terms of 'well-being'.

Welfare has been defined as the state of an animal as it attempts to cope with its environment (see Box 2.3) (Fraser and Broom, 1990), but Webster (1994) found this somewhat 'self referential' and preferred: 'the welfare of an animal is determined by its capacity to avoid suffering and sustain fitness'. The latter, however, focuses on what determines welfare and still leaves the term to be defined.

Ewbank (1999) has recently discussed all this in a very helpful chapter in the revised Universities Federation for Animal Welfare (UFAW) Farm Handbook and has suggested that 'there is practical merit in replacing the word "welfare" by the term "health and well-being"'.

FAWC, recognizing that welfare can be good or bad, defines its objective as positive welfare, going beyond the absence of cruelty (which is against the law in the UK) and assessed with reference to the Five Freedoms. Essentially, therefore, positive welfare can be defined as the state of well-being associated with satisfaction of the basic needs identified in Box 2.1.

Box 2.2 *Discussion of the term 'Natural'*

It is sometimes argued that if something is 'natural' it is acceptable or even good. However, a moment's reflection shows how wrong this may be.

Many of the most virulent poisons are perfectly 'natural'; fleas were once quite 'natural' inhabitants of human bodies, and even horrible diseases cannot really be described as 'unnatural'.

Behaviour that is natural in some circumstances may be regarded as quite 'unnatural' in others.

In the Five Freedoms, essential behaviour is described as 'normal', but the word 'natural' is sometimes used. However, this is not what makes it good or desirable. Either word is used to describe behaviour that is so characteristic of a species that its welfare is adversely affected if it cannot engage in it.

The 'natural' or 'normal' behaviour of many human beings is totally unacceptable, involving cruelty to others (people and animals), abuse, corruption, unethical behaviour and injustice. Children are encouraged to 'behave well' and discouraged from unkind or antisocial behaviour.

Pets are also discouraged from normal behaviour, such as scratching by cats, chewing furniture by puppies, aggression by pet dogs towards people and other animals, excretion in inconvenient places, mating by dogs in public places and a host of other perfectly 'natural' activities.

This also illustrates two other important features:

1 Behaviour early in life may influence later behaviour.

In poultry, for example, birds that are reared without perches may fail to find them when later kept in 'percheries' or 'aviary' systems. Indeed, they may fail to find feed and water placed on platforms. Other examples relate to the effect of early behaviour (eg dust-bathing) on later feather-pecking.

2 We accept the validity of training in early life to modify behaviour in ways that fit the subject for the life-system within which it is going to live. In the case of farm animals, since they are subject to genetic selection anyway, it is quite acceptable to select for or against undesirable habits.

Hens, for example, can be selected for a predisposition to low or high feather-pecking. This has to be done with caution, because there may be linkages with other traits. Such selection would really be aimed at fitting birds to the relatively crowded conditions of modern life.

In the case of pets, early training of dogs is commonplace but much less so for cats (limited to negative influences, such as not damaging furniture or excreting indoors) and hardly at all for other pets. Ponies are more appropriately thought of as companion animals rather than 'pets'.

But the idea of selecting genetically for 'good' habits and against 'bad' ones initially sounds repellent. However, it has been happening for a very long time, which is how we come to have breeds of dogs that are aggressive or gentle or good at retrieving, pointing, hunting and sheep or cattle herding, for example.

The difficulties are immediately apparent from the frequent use of the undefined word 'adequate'. One of the Five Freedoms is freedom from hunger and this serves to illustrate the problem (see Box 2.4).

We have recognized that more detailed criteria are needed, related to species, age, sex and weight for example (see Box 2.5), but do all these apply to all animals? This is an important question, since most of us would find it impracticable, and probably unreasonable, to have to avoid injuring, for example, the ants, aphids and caterpillars in our gardens. In any case, we do not even know that many of them are there and agriculture and gardening would be impossible without action to control pests.

If we are to think in terms of all living things, we have also to include plants. It is instructive to consider why most of us would not include plants, although there are senses in which we do concern ourselves with their welfare.

We would probably not refer to the well-being of plants, however, even though we know that some plants can 'feel' – in the sense that they respond to touch (very noticeable in species such as Mimosa). The key question, for all living things, as Jeremy Bentham pointed out, is not can they reason or talk but 'can they suffer?' So, in general, we do not believe that plants suffer and, however much suffering may occur in wild populations of animals, we are only concerned if we are involved, either by our action or our inaction.

Box 2.3 *Discussion of the term 'Coping'*

The term 'coping' usually refers to the ability to adapt or contend with a situation, and this is greatly aided if the situation is predictable. If animals are expecting events, they are usually better able to cope, though this seems unlikely if the event involves great suffering.

Indeed, it has been found that coping with stress can be learned. For example, pigs used in experiments to assess the stress of transport could only be used once (van Putten and Elshof, 1978). Subsequent stress was only a fraction of what was experienced on the first occasion, simply because the obstacles had become predictable. This observation clearly has a number of interesting implications, but predictability can work both ways. For example pigs may associate the noise of someone entering the building as indicating feeding time and, if that does not follow, stress (accompanied by a great deal of noise) can occur.

A second element in coping is the capacity to control or respond to events. If animals can avoid stressful events (by hiding or escaping) they are better able to cope. If they cannot, as with a barren environment and total lack of stimulation, they will invent responses, such as stereotypies (see Box 5.1). These repeated patterns of behaviour cause the production of morphine-like substances ('endorphins') in the brain, which dull perception and make life more tolerable. They are, however, addictive, and stereotypies may therefore continue even when the environment is improved.

One common cause of stress is mixing animals that have not met before: fighting may then occur to establish a 'pecking order'. On the other hand, established groups may actually help in coping. For example, pigs being loaded up a steep ramp that they have not encountered before, learn from each other. That is one reason why it is nearly always easier to move or drive a group of animals than one on its own. Yet it is important that an individual in a group can withdraw: there is a need for privacy.

Stress can be caused by depriving animals of the opportunity to behave normally, and the needs are not always obvious. For example:

1 A calf needs to suck and not just fill its stomach: a young calf may make 2500 sucking movements within a 24-hour period.
2 A sow not only needs a farrowing nest but needs to check its suitability by vigorous explorative behaviour.
3 A sow prefers to build its own nest with plenty of straw available, without which it does not feel 'safe'.

Box 2.4 *Hunger*

Freedom from hunger must have as its object the avoidance of an 'unacceptable' degree of hunger, rather than of any very short-term sensation. But there are husbandry systems that involve levels of feed supply, as essential and deliberate practice, which are much less than the animals would wish. Here are three examples:

1 Broiler breeders
The six million broiler breeders in the UK produce the eggs required by those rearing chickens for meat. These commercial broilers are grown at a rate close to their genetic potential, so that they reach market weight (2.4kg) by 42 days of age. The breeding birds naturally possess the same growth potential, but growth has to be controlled so that both males and females are at the optimum weight for breeding. Feed levels are therefore restricted and the birds are presumably hungry. However, in practice, it seems that both extreme restriction and ad lib feeding are unacceptable and a degree of control of feed intake that allows birds to grow at a steady rate is necessary.

2 Fish farming
Many species of fish cease to eat quite naturally in preparation for spawning, and all fish, being cold-blooded, will greatly reduce feed intake at low temperatures. It is not uncommon for salmon and trout in the wild to go without food for long periods, for example over winter, and when salmon return to freshwater, after a long migration, adults may cease feeding altogether for periods up to one year.

3 Breeding ewes
The natural breeding season of sheep is governed by day-length, resulting in early pregnancy coinciding with low feed supplies (early winter in the UK). Before this, however, just prior to mating, fertility is improved if the ewes are on a rising plane of nutrition (known as 'flushing'). Thus the breeding ewe does not require the same feed intake at all times and restrictions are necessary at times: it happens in nature and has to be arranged within a husbandry system.

Box 2.5 *Examples of Welfare Needs Specific to Animal Type*

Animal type	*Specific needs*
Species	Cows and hamsters clearly need different amounts of space. Some species are gregarious, others are solitary. Different species need different foods and vary in their need for water. Feeding frequency also varies: small mammals (eg mice and shrews) may need to feed every few hours, whereas pythons may feed only every few weeks.
Age	Older animals are usually heavier and stronger: the young may need to be protected against accidental crushing, even when the older animal is the suckling mother (eg pigs).
Sex	Sex ratios vary with species (eg one bull to 40 cows), so kept animals must be grouped accordingly. In some species, both sexes only come together at mating, and for the rest of the time live apart (eg weasels and bears). Others pair for life and pine if kept alone (eg gerbils)
Weight	Weight and size have a big effect on the need for food, water, heat and ventilation.

This suggests that we do not wish to include *all* animals but only those for which we feel some responsibility, because we keep them, control them or affect them in some way. And within this group, we limit our concern to 'sentient' animals – those that can suffer. Of course, we then have to define 'suffering' and devise ways of determining which animals are sentient and which are not. This is further explored in Chapter 3.

Some people hold that animals have rights, which we should respect. The same problems are associated with this position: if all animals are included, then it is probably necessary to recognize that they cannot all have the same rights. It is hard to find a meaningful way of expressing equal rights for ants and elephants, for example.

There is little doubt in most people's minds that animals can suffer: whether they do so in given circumstances may be less sure.

It has been said (Mellor, 1998) that doubts on the issue 'imply – unreasonably – that animals, unlike people, must prove that they can suffer before their suffering can be acknowledged'. It is surely suffering that we wish to avoid inflicting, causing or being responsible for. It is more humane to assume that sentient animals can suffer when placed in sufficiently adverse circumstances. The definition of 'sentient' is dealt with in Chapter 3.

Whatever disagreements there are about non-sentient animals, there will probably be fairly general agreement that we should be concerned about the welfare of sentient animals. There would therefore seem to be two main possible starting positions for thinking about animal welfare – two alternative ethical propositions from which to start:

1   Sentient animals have rights that should not be infringed.
2   Anyone who keeps sentient animals (or even knowingly affects them by his or her actions) thereby acquires a responsibility for their welfare.

Animal Rights

Many people are attracted by the proposition that animals have rights: others object strongly to this. The debate would be transformed if we simply changed this to 'animals should have rights'. This would also help to focus our minds on the following questions:

1   Do rights apply to all animals? (eg ants or dead animals?)
2   Does it mean that animals should therefore be free to exercise these rights? (All pets and pests have their freedoms constrained and it is hard to see how this could be otherwise.)
3   If animals should be able to exercise their rights, is this in all circumstances? (When a poisonous snake is about to strike you?)
4   What are these rights? And are they the same for all animals? (Surely not: the right to swim is not the same for an elephant and a fish.)

So, in its simplified form, I do not find this proposition helpful, though I can understand its appeal. In general, it means that some animals should be regarded as having some rights. The most obvious 'right' would be the right to life.

But what can this mean in a world where predators live by killing prey and every living thing has to die? Death cannot be avoided and most of us would rather put down an animal that was suffering and could not be cured, than allow it to continue in pain. If we contemplate a predator/prey relationship, such as an owl and a mouse, what rights does the owl have? To survive, it has to eat the mouse: so what rights does the mouse have? And however we answer these questions, what are we going to do about it? What is the meaning of rights that we will or can do nothing to protect? In the case of the owl and the mouse, the tiger and the antelope, the fox and the rabbit, we cannot, in any event, protect both.

The arguments are not dissimilar for humans, and my conclusion is that rights have to be conferred by a society prepared to protect them. It is quite legitimate to argue that certain animals ought to have rights conferred upon them and there is no reason to argue that such rights must be accompanied by responsibilities (babies, the very old and many sick people would be excluded thereby). However, in human relations we always expect that individuals exercising their rights must respect the legitimate rights of others. For all these reasons, I prefer the second proposition, which relates to our responsibilities toward animals and which can probably be accepted by everyone.

Human Responsibilities

If we accept that part of our responsibility when we keep animals, for whatever reason, is to ensure their well-being, we need to know what constitutes good welfare for that particular animal, what its needs are and how they can best be met. In this book, we can only deal with general principles: the detail required to look after all the different kinds of animals we keep and affect is enormous. It almost requires a whole book on each species and, of course, such books are often available and many of the welfare organizations also produce advisory leaflets (see Chapter 6). It is a perfectly clear responsibility on anyone who deals with animals to know how to look after them: sadly, this is not always the case (see Chapter 4) and cruelty is often caused by ignorance. That is an individual responsibility for individual behaviour and action.

Rather more difficult is our responsibility as citizens for the behaviour and standards of our society and for the actions of all its members. Here, individual action is more difficult and the help of an organization may be needed. It is thus also part of our responsibility to know what organizations exist and how to contact them. Chapter 6 lists most of the organizations in the UK and the more prominent ones internationally, but the total number, world-wide, is very large (about 6000). Appendix 2 gives details of how to make contact with such organizations and how to find out more about them.

It may also be part of our responsibility to press government for legislation: again, organizational support may be necessary. But, in any case, it is essential to be very clear what changes one is calling for. It is often relatively easy to identify a problem and only too easy to identify an apparent solution. After all, one cure for a headache would be to cut your head off! Solutions have to be workable, with the people and circumstances that are there, and must not give rise to other, possibly worse problems.

The FAWC confronts this difficulty all the time. It is against all mutilations (eg beak-trimming of poultry, tail-docking of pigs, castration of male farm animals and many others) but has to recognize that banning any one of them today might actually lead to worse welfare problems tomorrow. Beak-trimming may be necessary to prevent feather-pecking and cannibalism, tail-docking in pigs may prevent tail-biting and castration avoids fighting and unwanted reproduction. In the long run, the hope must be that systems of husbandry can be devised that will render these practices unnecessary. So we have to adjust our solutions to the time-scale and, it turns out, to a host of other factors.

If we are to influence government policy for the better, we have to think clearly about highly contentious and complicated issues that are emotionally charged and require a great deal of knowledge, not all of which may be available. Specific policies have to be tailored to specific cases and the context in which they occur. But, at this point, it is worth considering whether there are any general principles that can be used to guide our thinking and attitudes towards such specific cases.

The following questions are a sample of those that can or should be posed, and to which we as individuals should have an answer. Since the aim of this book is to help the reader to form conclusions, each question is followed by a proposition which suggests the form an answer might take so that you have something to challenge, to see whether you agree and, if not, how you would change it.

Rights and responsibilities

Question 1 To what animals does the concept of animal welfare apply?

Proposition 1 The welfare of sentient animals is a responsibility of those whose activities affect them. This is clear for those who affect them directly (by ownership, control, hunting, companionship, farming, transport, marketing, slaughter and association with recreation). Indirect effects are a more difficult area, partly because those affecting animals may not even be aware that they are doing so, partly because the effect may be remote in time or space and partly because such responsibility may clash with others (eg driving into a fox in order to avoid a child).

The slaughtering of animals

Question 2 What are the ethical responsibilities associated with animal slaughter?

As pointed out earlier, death is inevitable, so the main welfare concern must be that death should involve minimal suffering. Methods of humane slaughter have been worked out for the main farm animals, but no one method is equally appropriate for all species.

The same has to be said about the circumstances surrounding and leading up to death. Animals vary in relation to their sensitivity to restraint, transport, exposure to the slaughter of others including conspecifics, handling, noise, smell and a host of other factors. Shooting in the field may be better for some animals such as deer, whereas isolation, restraint and control may be best for others such as cattle, and stunning prior to slaughter may be a requirement.

Proposition 2 The method of slaughter, and the circumstances surrounding and leading up to death, should be appropriate to the animal and should be designed to minimize suffering.

As far as the animal is concerned, the reason for slaughter is irrelevant – it neither knows nor cares. However, there is an ethical issue for humans related to the reasons and justifications for the killing of animals, with killing for pleasure at one end of a scale (which many would regard as clearly wrong) and self-defence at the other (completely justified – sometimes independent of the method employed). This has nothing to do with animal welfare, however.

There is nonetheless one other welfare consideration, related to the age of the animal. The painless killing of a very old animal may even be regarded as an act of kindness, but the slaughter of day-old chicks or week-old calves raises greater difficulties, however painlessly it is done. The issue is whether the animal has been given a reasonable opportunity to 'enjoy' its life before losing it. The fact that this commonly happens in nature does not affect the argument, put by some, that deliberately bringing these animals into the world only to be slaughtered is wrong. It may be said that the animal can know nothing of what it is being deprived of and the alternative, of not producing it at all, does not solve the problem. The objection is largely based on a feeling that animals should not be regarded only as existing for our benefit or pleasure, even where that is their primary purpose, but that there should be some regard to their benefit and quality of life.

Suffering

Question 3 Is it wrong to cause or allow avoidable suffering to animals?

The importance of this question varies with culture and circumstances, including whether other priorities supervene. Clearly, during war or natural disasters, animals may be neglected in favour of, for example, children. It can be argued that, in these cases, the animal's suffering is, for practical purposes, unavoidable. Cultural differences do not have the same validity.

It may also be objected that we cannot accept responsibility for animals we do not own, control or affect. Animal welfare organizations, however, exist in order to bring about improvements in the behaviour of others. Insofar as ethics is about the rules governing societies, we clearly do have a responsibility to ensure their application beyond our own personal areas.

However, it should be noted that 'suffering' is a complex concept and may be quite different in relation to specific contexts. As Marion Dawkins (1998) has pointed out, 'suffering from grief' and 'suffering from hunger' are really so different as to have little in common. It is not to be expected, therefore, that there will be one, or even a few, key indicators.

Proposition 3 We should seek to minimize the avoidable suffering of animals to the extent that we have the power to do so as enshrined in UK law (see Box 2.6).

Box 2.6 *UK Law on the Protection of Animals*

Basically, to cause unnecessary pain or unnecessary distress to any livestock on agricultural land is an offence under section 1(1) of the Agriculture (Miscellaneous Provisions) Act of 1968. The breach of a code provision, whilst not an offence in itself, can nevertheless be used in evidence as tending to establish the guilt of anyone accused of the offence of causing unnecessary pain or distress under the Act (Section 3(4)).

1 The Protection of Animals Acts 1911–88 (in Scotland, the Protection of Animals Acts 1912–88) contain the general law relating to cruelty to animals. Broadly it is an offence (under Section 1 of the 1911 and 1912 Acts) to be cruel to any domestic or captive animals by anything that is done or omitted to be done.

2 Section 12(2) of the 1911 Act (Section 11(2) of the Scotland Act), empowers a police constable to place in safe custody, animals in the charge of persons apprehended for an offence under the Act until the end of proceedings or the court orders the return of the animals. The reasonable costs involved, including any necessary veterinary treatment, are recoverable by the police from the owner upon conviction.

3 Under Section 1 of the Protection of Animals (Amendment) Act 1954, as amended by the 1988 Act, the court has the power to disqualify a person convicted under these Acts from keeping animals. The ban can specify a particular kind of animal or all animals for such period as the court thinks fit. Where such a ban is imposed, the court can suspend the disqualification for such period as it thinks necessary to allow the person time to enable him to make suitable arrangements for the custody of any animals to which the disqualification relates.

There is a further question, to be addressed under the heading of animal welfare, related to the purposes for which animals are kept.

Many people object to animals being used at all: they tend to describe this as exploitation. I think it is worth distinguishing between the two. A human example makes the difference quite clear. We may use people (eg to help us in one way or another) but exploiting them implies ill-treatment or inadequate reward in situations where they do not have an effective choice. The same distinction seems valid for the use of animals.

As has already been said, what matters to the animal is whether it suffers: the human purpose behind an activity is almost irrelevant. But there may be grey areas, for example, where some suffering is inevitable but is justified, by those inflicting it, as being for the general good.

Sometimes, as in much medical research, suffering can be minimized or even avoided but, in other cases, the object of the experiment or test is to see whether the animal does suffer – in order to avoid using substances on humans that might cause suffering to them. Examples include the LD_{50} (Lethal Dose 50) tests for toxicity, which measured the dose that killed 50 per cent of the animals (to do this, doses would normally have to include those that killed more than 50 per cent) and the 'Draize' test for ophthalmic irritancy, in which drops of, for example, shampoo were put into the eyes of rabbits. Further examples are where there may be no physical suffering, and even no evidence of mental suffering either, but the animal is, in some sense, degraded.

The use of animals for entertainment illustrates the range of possibilities. Clearly, some examples such as bear- and badger-baiting and cock- and dog-fighting involve suffering and are unacceptable to most people.

The keeping of animals for exhibition (eg in zoos, aquaria, dolphinaria) may cause suffering and distress, due to lack of space, enforced training, or interference with communication systems (eg with a dolphin's sonar in small pools). But what of the cases where an animal is made to look ridiculous? Dressing a dog in fancy clothing, even clipping its coat in fancy patterns, may be accompanied by great care and affection (and inappropriate feeding), but does the animal suffer, or even care? Is it even aware of what we perceive?

Question 4 Is the degradation of animals wrong?

Some people may dislike it, find it embarrassing and regard it as pathetic or even unacceptable *human* behaviour, but does it have anything to do with animal welfare? And is it wrong? Some methods of keeping farm livestock may also appear degrading.

Proposition 4 Whilst we do not know the effect on the animal, treatment that may be regarded as degrading or significantly damaging to the animal's identity should be avoided, especially if it has no purpose other than human pleasure or amusement.

Interactions Between Environment and Animal Welfare

Strictly speaking, these subjects are very closely interlinked. Animals are part of our environment and one species may be part of the environment of another. The behaviour of all species is also a component of the environment.

If we wish to sustain a species, we have to sustain its habitat. Similarly, the best way to protect species diversity is to protect the diversity of habitats. However, conflicts do occur, mainly where the interests of one group of people require the control or even elimination of other species. This may be for reasons of health and disease control, to allow a preferred use of land as in farming or forestry or to avoid pests and irritants such as wasps. Sometimes this is mistaken or unnecessary, based on ignorance, or because no satisfactory compromise can be envisaged. But provided the methods of control are humane, there is no issue of animal welfare.

Mostly, such conflicts involve wild animals that are transient but damaging, as with geese on farmers' pastures, or animals that are too numerous for the environment to sustain, as with wild ponies of New Zealand or elephants in some parts of Africa. The latter poses an ethical dilemma in that control may involve killing and associated stress, whilst standing aside may lead to a painful natural balance being established, with damage to the environment and suffering to the animals. Natural balances may take time to establish and may often involve peaks and crashes of populations.

The first course of action involves interference – but we interfere in most directions most of the time – and the possibility of curtailing suffering. The second course leaves nature to sort itself out, as we generally do anyway for small species of animals. It is when the animals, such as elephants and horses, are noticeable that we perceive a problem, and the issue is most acute when our actions elsewhere (for example by drainage, destruction of migration routes or the total area available and the destruction of natural predators) have created the problem. No generalizations are possible and each case has to be considered on its own merits. But if the problem has been created by human action, interference seems to be the more logical option.

This leads to the final question and proposition.

Question 5 Is it right to interfere when the welfare of wild animals and the interests of the environment are in conflict?

Proposition 5 The possibility of creating such conflicts should be considered when altering environments: if human action has created conflict, there is a strong case for humane intervention.

It would be a useful exercise for anyone interested in animal welfare to develop some of these questions and propositions further or to extend the number to cover areas that ought to be included. Clearly, they could be developed by splitting them into more detailed questions, relating for example to particular species or actual issues, but there may be merit in this hierarchical approach, because the closer you get to a real-world issue, the more involved you become in personal emotions, biases and preferences. The value of the hierarchical approach is that it focuses first on the underlying principles, with which more detailed questions should accord.

Why does welfare matter?

This whole book assumes that animal welfare does matter and there may be little disagreement about such a general proposition. There is much less agreement when it comes to more detailed cases and what should be done about them. Such matters form the substance of later chapters, but it is important at the outset to be clear about why it matters. The following are the more obvious reasons:

1 *Because it is morally right to be concerned*
I use the term morals in relation to the values of individuals and ethics to refer to the values accepted by society. Both have been dealt with earlier in this chapter (but see Box 2.7).

2 *Because it is a responsibility of the citizen of any enlightened country*
The responsibilities of the citizen were covered in Chapter 1 (Box 1.2). The reason for some caution in describing a country as 'enlightened', 'advanced' or 'developed' is simply to recognize that societies vary in their ability to practise good animal welfare.

Societies that may only be able to survive by hunting wild animals (eg the Inuit) do not have the same choices as those of, for example, Western Europe. Countries that are extremely poor will understandably have higher priorities than animal welfare. If people are starving, there is little scope for concern for animals. It is true that in developed countries, poor and hungry people are to be found, but this is not because society cannot afford to do anything about it: it is due to a failure of will, generosity or the skill to devise workable or acceptable solutions.

3 *Because, to some degree, legislation requires it*
The law tends to provide a safety net, simply outlawing cruelty and ensuring minimal standards of welfare. As will be argued later (see Chapter 8), this may be inevitable and even preferable, since legislation is rather a blunt weapon for changing attitudes and other ways may be better and more effective.

Many countries have legislation (see Cooper, 1987, for the UK situation) covering the welfare of farm animals particularly, but the law also covers zoo animals, pets, some wild animals and others. In the European Community the Council of Europe has adopted a Convention for the Protection of Animals kept for farming purposes and the Commission's objectives are stated as 'the improvement of the welfare of animals from which we profit and for which we bear the responsibility of care'.

4 *Because individual action can effect change*
Public opinion and the behaviour of the public (as consumers of products and entertainment, as observers and as recipients of

education) can exert pressure on practitioners, other consumers and legislators, sometimes directly, sometimes via the media, pressure groups, unions, organizations or retailers.

This touches on who or what are the agents of change and how they should be deployed. These issues are discussed in detail in Chapter 7.

Box 2.7 *Ethics*

The ethical values accepted by society (so-called 'Rule-based ethics') evolve over time, often in quite radical ways, and yet they usually relate to what (at the time) are judged to be *ideal* situations and behaviour patterns. They do not describe 'how it is' but 'how it ought to be'. We wish to approach this ideal but we recognize that it often cannot be realized under present circumstances.

The moral relevance of 'naturalness' has been discussed in a Report by the Dutch Society for the Protection of Animals (DSPA, 1996). It was argued that animals have 'intrinsic value', measurable by their independence in relation to Man. This is most purely shown in wild animals and is inevitably compromised in animals used by Man. Of course, wild animals are not independent of almost anything else in their environment and it can be argued that the intrinsic worth of a person is actually reinforced by interdependence with others in structured communities.

The ethical responsibility, it could be argued, is to ensure that intrinsic worth is not subject to intolerable erosion when animals are used by Man.

Summary

1 Good welfare is not just the absence of cruelty.
2 Good welfare involves meeting the animals' needs for food, water, shelter, space, contact with others and providing the opportunity to express natural behaviour patterns.
3 Animals' needs all vary with species, sex, size and weight.

4   Since death is inevitable, concern for welfare has to focus on minimizing the suffering involved in it.

5   We have to recognize that real conflicts of interest arise between different animals, between animals and people and between animals and the environment.

3

All Animals – or Only Some?

'Everybody is important and nobody is very important' (Stephen Edberg)

In the last chapter, we discussed how widely our proper concern for animal welfare should be spread and concluded that, for practical purposes, it was sensible to focus on sentient animals – those capable of suffering. It was pointed out that much then depends on the meaning attached to 'suffering'.

Suffering

For our purposes, the dictionary definitions are too wide: they include 'undergoing or enduring', 'feeling pain', 'sustaining loss'. Now, a man can sustain a loss of money, but this does not necessarily involve suffering. A lizard will voluntarily detach its tail, in order to escape a predator. It has certainly suffered the loss of its tail but has it suffered? In any event, it grows a new one, so the loss is a temporary one. But is it relevant that the action is voluntary? Trapped animals may bite through a limb in order to escape: surely they suffer nonetheless? People may continue on a walking tour with badly blistered feet: suffering is surely independent of the reasons for it? The idea that welfare is chiefly related to the ability to cope with stress leads to the view that either suffering only occurs when an animal is unable to cope with stress or that suffering does not necessarily mean poor welfare.

The way out of this dilemma is to draw lines between degrees of suffering. A pig chewing an iron bar, a horse repeatedly swaying its head, or a caged tiger pacing up and down (behaviour known as 'stereotypies') are coping with stress but may still be suffering. In the same way, one may cope perfectly well with a broken leg or a visit to the dentist, but it does not mean that there is no suffering or that welfare is fine. People who wish to slim may deliberately go hungry; others fast to achieve desired states of mind. Animals must feel hunger as a stimulus to feeding. So the degree or duration of hunger seems to be relevant.

One could go on describing what appear to be anomalies, simply because 'suffering' is somewhat subjective. This may lead to the view that objective, scientific tests are needed. Indeed, Professor Des Fielden, for many years Chair of the New Zealand Animal Welfare Advisory Committee, considers that there is a desperate need to find practical methods of measuring pain and distress objectively.

These may take the form of physiological tests, such as analyses of blood constituents, or of rigorous observation of features, especially behaviour, that are known to be associated with suffering. In many cases, most of us do not require anything more than observation to judge whether an animal or a person is suffering – and we may mostly be right. But what happens when, as in some sports, opinions differ radically: one person 'knows' that the animal suffers, another 'knows' that it does not.

There are also many grey areas where it is hard to be certain whether animals suffer or not. Sometimes this is because there may be few outward signs. As mentioned in Chapter 1, some animals deliberately disguise injury: others feign it (as in birds that try to distract predators from finding their nests). We often judge from the expressions on people's faces, but many animals have only a limited capacity for facial expression: birds, because of the structure of their faces, have virtually none. Vocalization is also a common key, but a dumb person is just as capable of suffering, and if you have ever tried to recover a bantam hen from a tree in order to put it in a safe roosting place, you will be quite familiar with the combination of very gentle handling and penetrating screeching that suggests that murder most foul is being done.

My conclusion is that suffering involves the feeling (awareness) of pain, injury or acute discomfort (including mental discomfort), and that one cannot usefully generalize about how to detect it. The focus on feeling supports the distinction between sentient and non-sentient animals.

Sentience

Rather obviously, the way in which sentience is defined determines which animals fall into the category of sentient beings and which do not. Some dictionary definitions simply specify 'responsive to stimuli', but this would include all animals and probably all plants. Other definitions add 'aware', and this implies a mind, such that the whole organism can be aware of something, as distinct from, say, one part of the organism reacting to a stimulus.

In the previous two chapters, I have used 'sentience' to imply 'capable of suffering' and, in the sense in which I have used 'suffering', a mind capable of feeling is implied. So I propose to use 'sentience' to mean 'capable of suffering because of an ability to feel pain, injury and discomfort, and to be aware that these sensations matter'.

Sentient and Non-Sentient Animals

Consistent with the above definition, scientists tend to judge sentience by assessing the degree of development of the central nervous system. Broadly speaking, all vertebrates (mammals, birds, reptiles, amphibians, fish) are judged to be sentient and most invertebrates (eg insects, crustaceans, spiders, snails, shellfish) are judged to be non-sentient (although concern is often expressed at the way in which lobsters, oysters and snails are killed, on the grounds that it seems clear that they are suffering – at least in some cases).

There are exceptions, however, and the demarcation line is not immutable. A few years ago, for example, the octopus was reclassified as sentient following detailed studies on its nervous system, (Bateson, 1992) and many people now feel that crustaceans, especially lobsters, are capable of feeling pain.

The main guidelines for the division between 'sentient' and 'non-sentient' animals are the presence or absence of relevant structures and physiological processes and the presence or absence of aversive behaviour. The absence of a cerebral cortex or of nerve pathways and chemical transmitters normally linked to pain transmission would indicate the absence of a capacity to suffer in 'lower' animals.

This distinction seems to be helpful but there is still room for considerable argument. For example, invertebrates may be behaving instinctively even though their behaviour appears superficially to be intelligent and even thoughtful. Yet if circumstances are only slightly changed, an insect seems to be totally baffled and cannot adjust. Solitary wasps for example, may bring prey (spiders, caterpillars etc) and put them down whilst they uncover the entrance to their burrows (often on footpaths). If the prey is moved for only a short distance, the wasps will search where they left it but rarely identify it in its new position.

However, all animals, including ourselves, sometimes behave instinctively, but this does not mean that we do not also think. In fact, a great many lowly animals give every appearance of going beyond instinct at times: they investigate their surroundings and, after apparent thought, they make choices (for a discussion of this see Ford, 1999). So, if they can think, can they feel? Perhaps they can but it seems unlikely that they are aware of their feelings: this would require a degree of consciousness that such creatures are unlikely to possess.

There is little most of us could do about the welfare of invertebrates (although Buddhists try to include them) and we do not generally keep them as farm livestock, pets or companion animals. This is not entirely so, of course, since children keep stick insects and other creatures as pets and two species of insect – the honey bee and the silk moth – have been farmed for centuries. We also use crustaceans for food and the methods by which they are killed may be of concern. A good example is the killing of lobsters by dropping them into boiling water. This is certainly not an instantaneous death and the lobster does appear to suffer.

The increasing use of biological control – the use of one organism to control another regarded as a pest – means that many insects, such as ladybirds and parasitic wasps, are now bred in captivity and released, sometimes in the open, often in glasshouses, to prey on pest species. Any action against pests constitutes deliberate action to harm them and we show little concern about the method of destruction. So it is not the case that we do not affect non-sentient animals. We do, often with very worthy motives, as with the destruction of mosquitoes to control the spread of malaria.

Life would be very difficult if we extended the concept of 'suffering' to all living animals and no one would probably dissent from the view that concern should be concentrated on those that are sentient. But we cannot sensibly extend our concerns to all sentient animals and the ethical starting point proposed in Chapter 2 limited our responsibility to those sentient animals that we keep, control or affect (see Table 3.1).

Table 3.1 *The Main Species of Sentient Animals Used*

Category	UK	World (additional to those used in the UK)		
Farm livestock	Cattle, Goats, Sheep, Pigs, Poultry	Buffaloes, Camels, Horses, Donkeys, Ostriches, Monkeys		
Companion animals	Dogs, Cats, Ponies, Birds, Rabbits, Mice, Donkeys			
Captive animals	Large cats, Elephants, Monkeys, Bears, Birds, Reptiles, Amphibia			
Work	Horses, Dogs, Donkeys, Ferrets	Elephants, Mules, Cormorants, Llamas		
			Hunting	*Hunted*
Sport	Horses, Dogs, Hawks, Pigeons, Pheasants	Camels, Bulls, Whales, Pigs	Dogs, Hawks, Horses	Game birds, Pigs, Deer, Big game
Wild				
Hunting	Foxes, Deer,	Pigs,		
Shooting	Game birds	Large cats		
Laboratory animals	Rats, Mice, Monkeys, Dogs, Cats			

Animals Whose Welfare Should be Our Concern

The main groups can be delineated in no particular order of importance as follows:

• Farm livestock
• Companion animals (including pets)
• Captive animals
• Working animals
• Animals used for sport, recreation and entertainment
• Wild animals affected by man
• Animals used in experiments

It is immediately apparent that the same species (even the same
animal) can appear in more than one category: the horse can be
included in all of them, many pets are captive, wild animals may be
used for sport, and farm livestock may be captive, working and
companion. A sheepdog is a good example of an animal which may
be all of those things. It is also apparent that the species of animal
cannot be used to decide into which category it falls (though sometimes the breed can do so). What determines the category is the
way that they are used or even regarded: and the way that they are
used will usually reflect a purpose.

Farm Livestock

The main species used in world agriculture are listed in Table 3.1,
but the total list is closer to 25. A major characteristic of a farm
animal is that its reproduction is under human control. This is not
so for the cropping of wild populations, such as deep sea fish for
example. It follows that farm animals have to be confined or closely
herded, and a degree of responsibility taken for their feeding, watering and protection from predators and disease. Of course, not all
stages of production, including reproduction, necessarily take place
on the same farm.

  Equally, farm animals do not spend all their time on a farm,
although the major part of their lives will be there. But significant
numbers are transported, pass through markets and are slaughtered,
and welfare may be a major concern in all these cases.

  Fish are not listed in Table 3.1 and many people would not think
of them as farm animals. In fact, it is only recently (1997) in New

Zealand that fish have been included as 'animals' in the Animal Welfare Bill. However, they are farmed, in large numbers, and they raise some rather different welfare problems (see Box 3.1).

Box 3.1 *Fish Farming*

The farming of fish is relatively recent in the UK but, in the last 30 years, has expanded greatly: salmon, trout and carp are the main species involved.

In 1994, there were 119 salmon-producing companies in Scotland operating 262 sites and a further 68 ova and smolt companies on 147 sites. In Europe and, indeed, the world, the largest producer is Norway (with more than three times the UK output), and salmon farming also occurs on the west coast of Ireland, the Faroe Islands and, to a small extent, in France and Spain. Trout farming has been carried out on a small scale in the UK for over 100 years and in 1994 there were 373 registered trout farms. Carp farming is at its northern limit in the UK and the industry is small. Much of the carp produced on the 175 registered farms (1994) are destined for sport and ornamental ponds.

Good welfare requires an adequate supply of suitable water (marine for salmon) and freedom from disease (now mainly prevented by vaccination), disorders, injury and distress. The main welfare concerns are method of slaughter, starving prior to slaughter, and stocking rates, and these provide good examples of the need to understand the biology of the animal before jumping to conclusions about what is good welfare.

Stunning is essential prior to slaughter and currently the most humane method of stunning is clubbing (with a club called a 'priest'), followed by severing of the gills: properly done by trained (and not tired) operators, clubbing – unpleasant as it sounds – is the best way to stun and this is the most essential requirement. Other methods, for example of mechanical stunning and the use of CO_2, are being explored.

Prior to slaughter, salmon are often deprived of food for days or even weeks in order to empty the gut: FAWC recommends a maximum of 72 hours. Wild salmon cease feeding before breeding and are adapted to food deprivation at this time. However, whether regularly-fed farmed fish suffer from food deprivation is less certain.

Stocking rates clearly should not be too high, but fish tend to crowd together in a shoal and, in fact, it is recognized as a sign of good health when fish respond to disturbance by shoaling.

Companion Animals

Not all companion animals can be described as pets, and many pets are not really companion animals. Companionship implies rather more than living in the same household: it suggests some degree of interaction between animal and human. But there are lots of marginal cases where the distinction is not clear-cut and would look different to different people.

There are also animals that are kept almost as part of the scenery. For example, deer in the park of a big country house, goldfish in a garden pond, and peacocks. They are not exactly captive, although they are certainly confined, and they can hardly be called recreational or wild.

All this reinforces the notion that these categories simply represent a useful framework for discussing the needs and welfare of animals, but they do not affect our responsibilities towards them. The purposes for which they are kept, however, may impose some constraints on how they can be treated, the freedoms they can be given and the amount of attention they can receive.

Captive Animals

Most animals that are kept are captive to some degree, in that they are not free to go where they wish, without limit. But there are obvious examples, such as those confined in zoos and menageries, where the situation is clearly different from the other categories. Captive animals tend to be wild animals, many of which have to be contained for reasons of safety for humans and other animals. The number of species can be huge, depending on the zoo. In London Zoo, for example, the number of species of sentient animals in 1996 was about 650 (including: mammals 113 species, birds 130, reptiles 136, amphibians 66 and fish 154). The major problems relate to larger species since it is rarely possible to reproduce the natural environment, and especially its scale, or, in the case of predators, natural live prey. Modern zoos tend not to depend upon 'cages', as distinct from 'enclosures', and, in most cases, do not keep animals either on their own or in isolation. This cannot be said, of course, for all pets (eg budgerigars, canaries, snakes, goldfish, hamsters).

Some wild animals are kept captive for the production of valued substances. For example over 3000 wild civets are kept in Ethiopia for the production of musk; 1000kg of civet musk are exported to France each year for use in the perfume and cosmetic industry.

Working Animals

In developed countries, very few animals are still used for transport and of these some have additional purposes, such as publicity, associated with brewers' dray horses.

In developing countries, however, very large numbers of animals are used for work and especially for transport. Historically, some of these animals have been of enormous importance, particularly the horse and its military role (see Diamond, 1997), but increasingly they are displaced by machines, with an enormous reduction in animal suffering. The main animals used for work in agriculture are listed in Table 3.2.

Table 3.2 *Animals used for Work in Agriculture*

Type of animal	Main use
Horses, oxen, buffalo, elephant	Traction, cultivation and clearing of land
Horses, donkeys, mules, oxen, buffalo, llamas	Transport
Dogs	Herding
Insects, arachnids, ducks, geese, fish, amphibians	Biological control of insect pests and weeds
Bees	Pollination of flowers for fruit and seed

A similar process will probably happen for other uses of animals. For example, the use of 'sniffer' dogs to detect drugs, explosives and people is currently increasing, but such dogs take a great deal of care and expensive training and will probably be displaced by non-animal methods. The difficulty is in reproducing the dog's astonishing ability to detect and distinguish odours and sounds. The sensory abilities of lower animals (eg the ability of male moths to detect the scent-pheromones of females at distances of up to five miles) may provide better models for artificial systems.

The willingness of dogs to learn and to collaborate with humans has led to a wide range of uses, including herding (sheep and cattle), guidance for the blind, guarding and protection (of people, property and animals), and some of these activities expose the animals to danger. Other animals have been used in the past and displaced. For example, canaries were used by miners to detect gas. It is worth noting that some wild animals are used as pollution detectors (for example, fish in rivers and molluscs for heavy metals in coastal waters) but these are not yet deliberately placed or controlled, but are just sampled from the wild. Small numbers of birds are used to enhance safety on airfields and to rid public areas of nuisance pigeons: hawks of various kinds are the most commonly used. In London, for example, pigeons are discouraged but not killed by the Harris Hawk, a native of America.

Animals Used for Sport, Recreation and Entertainment

Animals used for sport, recreation and entertainment are listed in Table 3.3.

Where the Animal is not Harmed

This includes the racing of dogs, horses, camels, pigeons and, possibly, frogs. The animals involved are usually well cared for because their performance depends on their fitness and their value increases if they are successful. No harm is intended; however, abuses of the animal may occur in attempts to increase performance such as the excessive use of whips and spurs, and training methods, such as the breaking in of horses in dressage, may involve cruelty. At this point, it is important to recognize that cruelty may not be inherent in the activities or in the methods, but how and by whom they are practised. There are, for example, different methods of breaking in horses. Much cruelty to animals is not malicious but due to ignorance, callousness or thoughtlessness: as noted earlier, however, this makes no difference to the animal or its suffering. In some sporting activities, the animal is part of a partnership, such as riding and polo: it is a major difference between horse and dog racing, for example.

Where Harm is Intended

The most obvious examples in this category are hunting, shooting, some fishing and trapping.

Worldwide, a great many species are involved, most of them wild and therefore dealt with in the following section. The excep-

Table 3.3 *Animals used for Sport, Recreation and Entertainment*

---

1 *Where the animal is not harmed (apart from accidents)*

Racing	Horses, dogs, camels, pigeons
Jumping	Horses
Showing	Horses, cattle, sheep, pigs, hens, pigeons, rabbits, dogs, cats
Riding	Horses and ponies

2 *Where harm is intended*

Hunting	Deer, foxes, hares, wild boar, otters
Shooting	Deer, big game (eg lions, tigers, antelope, elephant, rhino), rabbits, game birds, wild birds
Fishing (for trophies)	Trout, salmon, carp
Fighting	Dogs, bears, badgers, cocks

3 *Where harm is not intended but may occur*

Angling (for release)
Dancing bears
Circus animals
Dolphinaria
Aquaria
TV performing animals

Note: Some would argue that there may be little difference between (1) and (3)

tions are where animals are bred in captivity and released for hunting or shooting. The most numerous examples are probably game birds (eg pheasants); even more may be essentially wild but in a managed environment in which they may even be protected from natural predators, as for example on grouse moors, and given supplementary food.

Some hunting involves animals other than the target species. Horses confer speed, on elephants the benefit is protection. Trained dogs are commonly used to trace, follow, wear down, corner and even kill the quarry. Their welfare is an additional concern.

Where Harm is not Intended
The best example in this category is angling in which caught fish are returned to the water. It can hardly be argued that no harm is

caused, since the fish are hooked, played, handled and confined in holding nets. The question is whether any or all of this causes suffering. Some people are less persuaded that cold-blooded animals feel pain, but the evidence is that they can, so we are left with the question as to whether they do, in the circumstances described.

Here it is worth pointing out that the fact that worse things happen to the animals in the wild has no real relevance. We cannot base our standards of behaviour to animals, or to other people, on what happens to them in other circumstances or on the way that other animals or people behave.

Animals used for entertainment are not usually intended to suffer, but positive welfare may not receive sufficient attention. There are notable exceptions, however. No one can pretend that no suffering is involved in bull-fighting, bear-baiting, badger-baiting, cock-fighting and dog-fighting, where the suffering is actually a part of the entertainment. Both in the UK and in the US, cruel practices such as dog- and cock-fighting have been banned (the latter since 1835 in the UK) but simply thrive underground.

Zoo animals are common examples of animals that are caged primarily for the entertainment of visitors, but where no suffering is intended. Education and conservation of species are becoming of increasing importance, but public exhibition is usual and an important source of revenue.

Many of the sporting activities already mentioned also serve entertainment purposes, but there are many cases of animals used for entertainment that have no sporting element at all. Dancing bears are a good example of entertainment where the cruelty is mainly involved in the unseen taming and training of the animals. They also illustrate some of the difficulties involved in doing anything about the problem. There are social problems: it will often be the case that the owner of the bear has no other means of earning a living. There are also animal welfare problems: what do you do with the damaged bear, even if you gain possession of it? These problems will be further discussed in Chapter 7.

There is also another dimension of the use of animals for entertainment. Does the exhibition of animals infringe their integrity and their dignity? Are they aware of this and does it matter? If so, what about the dressing up of pet dogs and monkeys? Do they think that they look ridiculous? It surely interferes with their ability to relate to other animals and they must feel it to be strange.

Wild Animals Affected by Man

Hunting, shooting and fishing have already been discussed, but there are other ways in which we affect wild animals. The effect may be deliberate, as in population control in conservation of animals or habitats, the control of pests or their simple exclusion from protected areas, farmland and gardens, which in some cases interferes with their migration routes.

But effects may not be deliberate at all. They may be accidental and unavoidable, as in crushing a hedgehog with a car or hitting a deer, or they may be due to ignorance, as in the disruption of wildlife by land development. In the latter case, it is only judged to matter if the animals are rare or legally protected. Otherwise, individual animals are unhurt and free to relocate elsewhere. However, it should not be thought that we only affect wild animals adversely or that we are only concerned about mammals and birds. In the UK, for example, there are schemes to rescue toads and frogs and to prevent them from being crushed on busy roads.

Animals Used in Experiments

This is one of the most contentious areas. Many people would prefer that live animals were not used in experiments, but the extent that such use is judged to be necessary or justified varies considerably. The evolution of attitudes and legislation in the UK has recently been reviewed by Moore (1999). Even where the experiments themselves cause no pain (eg when anaesthetics are used) there may be objections to the sacrifice of animals for such purposes – but is this fundamentally different from farming livestock for food or rearing animals for spare parts?

It is entirely understandable that people should be so concerned about human suffering and the possibility of learning how to avoid or cure it by carrying out experiments on animals that these appear justified. It is also entirely understandable that many people should feel that the relief of human suffering should not be at the price of the suffering of others, whether people or animals. Furthermore, there is no absolute guarantee that an animal experiment will actually lead to the alleviation of human suffering, even in the distant future. It is also argued that whilst animal experiments are allowed, the search for alternative methods will not be pursued with sufficient vigour. Such views may be strongly held even if the experiments are so conducted that animals do not physically suffer.

This is one of the most difficult areas in which to think clearly and it involves some human ethical considerations which are mixed up with those relating to animal welfare. The same is found in attitudes to hunting: it may be judged to be wrong, whether it involves animal suffering or not. A simple question illustrates the point: is it right or acceptable to pull the wings off flies even if it can be demonstrated that they feel no pain?

Summary

1   It is sensible to focus our concerns on sentient animals and on those we keep or affect by our actions.
2   We need to be careful in judging whether an animal is suffering or not. It is not always obvious and we need to avoid assuming that animals feel in the same way as we do.
3   The main groups of animals affected are farm livestock, companion animals, captive animals, working animals, those used for sport or entertainment, experimental animals and some wild animals.

4

The Nature and Scale of the Welfare Problem

'Ignorance is a voluntary misfortune'
(English proverb)

In spite of what has been said in previous chapters, the ordinary citizen would not need to be greatly concerned about animal welfare – except with regard to personal actions – if all was well and there were no serious problems.

However, that is not the case. Vast numbers of animals are involved, even in the UK, never mind the world, so that, even if the majority are well-treated, the remaining problem is huge. For example, it is estimated that, in the UK alone, 25 per cent of the 32 million laying hens suffer bone fractures – that is eight million each year. Furthermore, as with all suffering, only a small proportion is ever recorded or even known to more than those immediately involved. So, whilst recognizing that there are many individual cases, where individual remedial or preventive action may be possible, in this book we can only focus on principles and general practice.

Let us consider numbers of animals first. It does not follow that, because there are more animals involved, there is a bigger welfare problem, but the scale of the operation does have two important consequences. Firstly, if there *is* a welfare problem involved in the operation it is likely to be magnified. Secondly, the sheer scale of the operation constrains what can be done to improve animal welfare. This is well exemplified by slaughter (see later section).

The kind of problem can be illustrated in the hatching of chicks. The average incubation period is 21 days but some may hatch after 19 days. These latter have to wait from 24 to 48 hours for the rest to hatch and have to spend this time in the incubator at 37°C and a relative humidity of 75 per cent. They lose body fluid that they cannot yet replace and consume the remaining yolk that constitutes their food reserve. This may be followed by a long journey, possibly by air (see Box 4.4).

This problem derives to a considerable extent from the very large numbers involved. The numbers for the categories of animals described in Chapter 3 are shown in Tables 4.1, 4.2, 4.4, 4.5 and 4.6.

Farm Livestock

Table 4.1 *UK and World Farm Livestock*

Type of animal	Number (millions)	
	World	UK
Cattle (total)	1250	11
Sheep	1200	44
Buffaloes	137	–
Camels	19	–
Goats	592	0.075–0.1
Pigs	823–939	7
Poultry	10,000-13,000	126

Source: after Spedding, 1996 and others

The main welfare problems in the UK are not concerned with feeding, watering and shelter, except in very extensive systems where bad weather on the hills can cause death of sheep due to exposure, for example. During severe drought in Australia, however, losses due to lack of food and water may be enormous. Although losses tend to be higher in harsh environments, it is estimated that in the UK as a whole 10 to 25 per cent of all lambs born die within three days. Nor are the main problems generally related to disease, except that if disease does break out it may spread rapidly, due to the concentration of livestock, especially poultry and pigs.

It is part of the business of farming that these matters are covered in a scientific and controlled manner. That is not to say that there are no disease concerns: all diseases represent poor welfare and some of the most worrying are those that are chronic and may cause suffering over long periods.

There are also a number of unusual forms of farming which raise problems by their very nature. Here are three examples:

1   *Seal Farming*
    In the remote Russian village of Koida, it is reported (1994) that thousands of baby Harp seals were kept in pens to await killing after they had developed the prized spotted coats (which start at about three weeks old). The World Society for the Protection of Animals (WSPA) is promoting tourism, to view seals, as an economic alternative.

2   *Production of pâté de foie gras*
    This occurs in geese and ducks in France, Israel and mid-European countries such as Hungary and Poland. It is usually based on a seven-fold increase in liver size, caused by force-feeding of 400–500 grams of salted, cooked maize four times a day. Over a few weeks, the birds' weight is increased by some 60 per cent. It is estimated that, in France alone, 18 million caged ducks and 800,000 geese are force-fed each year.

3   *'Puppy Farming'*
    This is not really farming at all but does raise concerns (see Box 4.6).

The attention now paid to the welfare problems of farm livestock, owes much to the pioneering work of Ruth Harrison (1964) in her book *Animal Machines*. The most recent review of the subject is in the 1999 UFAW Farm Handbook.

In the main, the welfare problems of most farm livestock relate to constraints on space, causing overcrowding and limiting the animal's ability to express its normal behaviour patterns; methods of handling, especially in transport and at markets; methods of slaughter and mutilations.

Constraints on Space

The clearest examples of lack of space are laying hens in battery cages. Laying hens are currently allocated 450 sq cm per bird with three to five to a cage: FAWC recommends a minimum of 600 sq cm (see Box 4.1) and the European Commission (EC) is now proposing 800 sq cm. Clean water and feed, however, are constantly supplied and disease control is excellent.

Box 4.1 *Battery Cages for Hens*

In the UK, 84 per cent of laying hens are kept in cages, compared with 93 per cent in the European Union (EU) as a whole.

Battery cages are currently the most economic way in which to keep laying hens. They are good for most of the Five Freedoms but clearly do not (and cannot) satisfy the hen's need to express normal behaviour – however this is described. This is simply because the space allowed is too small: four birds are commonly kept in one cage and each has 450 sq cm. FAWC has long recommended a minimum of 600 sq cm and in 1998 the EC proposed that all new cages should provide 800 sq cm per bird from 1 January 1999, with all existing cages moved up to this level from 1 January 2009.

If this increases the cost of egg production in batteries, it will greatly narrow the gap between this and the cost of 'barn' or 'free-range' eggs. The worry for producers is that the new rules will not be enforced evenly across Europe, quite apart from competition from countries outside Europe. In the US, for example, it is reported that space allowances may be no more than 350 sq cm per bird. The objection to such practices is mainly because of the close confinement of the animals.

Some methods of pig production raise problems, especially sow stalls and tethers. Both were banned in the UK in 1999 and tethers will be banned in the EU from 2006. But beef cattle in feedlots may appear very crowded and free range poultry may be grossly overstocked, thus limiting the space available to each animal. Economic considerations (mostly involving capital investment) are the most important reasons for space restriction, but there are also often other reasons, such as ease of inspection by staff. Other animals including pets and smaller farmed animals are also kept in small cages. Rabbits, for example, are often kept in tiers of cages, much like battery cages for hens, with less legislative control than is applied to laboratory rabbits, although in the UK there are Ministry of Agriculture, Fisheries and Food (MAFF) recommendations about the minimal size of cages. The cage dimensions that are needed are not always obvious. For example, rabbits can only wash their faces properly when standing up on their hind legs. Cages must therefore be of adequate height. Rabbit farming for meat is a relatively small industry in the UK, although we still use more rabbits for meat than we do for research. In other countries such as Italy, cages may be much smaller and we import a great deal of the rabbit meat sold in Britain from the continent or even China. There is now a UFAW/RSPCA Rabbit Behaviour and Welfare Group to promote rabbit welfare. Cages are not the only forms of undesirable space restriction: narrow veal crates and Pregnant Mare Urine (PMU) farming also provide examples (see Boxes 4.2 and 4.3 respectively).

Methods of Handling

Handling may raise welfare problems wherever it occurs, but markets and transport are probably the areas of greatest concern.

Markets

Methods of handling can cause poor welfare where staff are poorly trained, poorly motivated, tired or impatient, and range from rough handling (by horns, tails, wool) to physical assault with sticks and electric prods. Poor handling is counter-productive and tends to become habitual in people who can no longer see anything wrong with it.

Transport

There are now EU regulations covering journey times, lorry design, feeding and watering and methods of loading, but it is hard to police them and to get them right. For example, in well-designed transport, loading and unloading cause more stress than travelling, yet an arbitrary limit on journey time may enforce a stop involving unloading, when another hour would have completed the journey (see Box 4.4).

The Canadian Federation of Humane Societies (CFHS) reports (1998) that spent laying hens typically are transported from 50 to 500 miles to the slaughter plant (18 hours for local journeys, 26 hours for interprovincial journeys) with no water, feed or temperature control. The Health of Animals Act allows cattle and sheep to be transported for up to 52 hours without feed and water, and pigs and horses for up to 36 hours.

Box 4.2 *Veal Crates*

Veal production, traditionally, meant the rearing of calves in narrow wooden crates, on liquid iron-deficient diets to produce 'white' veal, not as a cheap meat but to meet a demand for expensive, luxury food. These methods offend all of the Five Freedoms. Numbers reared in this way are diminishing, however. In the UK, narrow veal crates were effectively banned in 1990 but many young calves were then exported to be reared in this way in France or Holland. It is quite possible to rear veal calves humanely, so it is not necessary to ban the whole process.

In North America, veal production has been declining since its peak in the 1980s and by 1994 numbers of 'special-fed' calves were about 875,000; 'red' (grain-fed) calves were about 175,000; and 'bob' calves were about 500,000. Of these, some 725,000 male dairy 'special-fed' calves, about 110,000 non-special-fed and about 324,000 'bob' calves were reared in the US, with the remainder reared in Canada.

Box 4.3 *PMU Farms*

Pregnant Mare Urine (PMU) is used by the pharmaceutical industry for the production of a hormone replacement therapy (HRT) drug to alleviate symptoms of the menopause and to prevent osteoporosis in post-menopausal women.

Unfortunately, the mares used for this are often kept in tiny stalls with little opportunity for exercise and they are often short of water and veterinary supervision.

In Alberta, Saskatchewan, Manitoba and Dakota alone, there are more than 480 PMU farms and an estimated 75,000–80,000 pregnant mares are kept confined for more than six months at a time whilst their urine is collected.

Box 4.4 *Livestock Transportation in Europe*

In 1991, the European Directive 91/629 was introduced, which allowed the transport of livestock for up to 24 hours without a food or water break, with no proper definition of the rest period then required. A new Directive was intended to come into force on 1 July 1999, limiting journeys to eight hours unless vehicles of a defined standard (including ventilation or temperature control) were used. Criteria relating to loading and unloading and minimum standards for lairages have now been agreed. The UK has implemented this Directive in the Welfare of Animals (Transport) Order, 1997, but a number of other European countries have not. Furthermore, the Directive is being interpreted differently in different countries.

Transport by air may raise special problems. For example, day-old chicks may be exposed to life-threatening high temperatures, especially when the ventilation is switched off during take-off and landing.

There are some acute problems in handling: two examples will serve to illustrate them.

'Harvesting' for Transport

It is often difficult, tiring and exasperating to persuade large animals to move in a particular direction, and especially up a ramp. Equally, catching smaller animals, like poultry, can be very frustrating and human patience can easily become exhausted.

When meat birds are harvested for slaughter, they are commonly grabbed by the legs and three to ten per cent may be injured (bruises and bone fractures). Spent battery hens are often removed from their cages by one leg and carried, three at a time, to the transport crates: this too can result in bone fractures, especially of the wing bones. Meat ducks are grabbed by the neck and carried, two in each hand.

Machine harvesting often strikes people as inhuman simply because it is *non*-human, but this is precisely the advantage. Machines do not get tired or lose their temper: their performance is consistent. There are now excellent machines for gently moving poultry such as broilers on to a moving belt and thence to a vehicle or container. They do not frighten the birds and thus produce no panic. Broilers cooperate well, but turkeys do not, and this variation in the reaction of species needs to be continually borne in mind as in every other aspect of welfare.

Looking well into the future, there is even the possibility of mechanical 'herding' of animals, aimed at reducing the stress experienced by sheep, for example, during gathering. A 'robot sheepdog' has been under development for about three years in UK research institutes.

Removal of 'Spent' Hens

When battery hens have finished their productive lives, they have to be removed through the rather restricted opening in the front of the cage. This is most easily done by grasping their legs, but unfortunately, since battery hens do not exercise their legs much, their bones are rather brittle and broken legs can be a serious problem. Note that this is an example where injury does *not* affect production and weakens the farmers' argument that if they did not look after their animals they would not be productive.

Methods of Slaughter

The numbers of farm animals slaughtered annually are shown in Table 4.2. However, accurate world statistics are not available at all for some species and are not very reliable for others: it is clearly impossible to know about slaughter in households and villages across the world.

Table 4.2 *Numbers of Farm Animals Slaughtered Annually in the World for Meat*

	Animals slaughtered (millions)		Meat production (million tonnes)	
	1979–81	1988	1979–81	1988
Beef and veal	223.3	236.5	44.1	48.1
Mutton and lamb	385.2	442.0	05.7	06.6
Goat	159.9	197.5	01.8	02.4
Pork	735.8	870.5	51.5	64.4

Source: after Pickering, 1992

In the UK and most advanced countries, methods of slaughter of farm animals are controlled by law and the great advantage of large abattoirs is that they can be readily inspected and monitored. The disadvantages include the resulting greater distances from farm to abattoir.

Humane Killing

Animals of all species may have to be killed, whether planned as in farming or as a result of accident, injury, disease or debilitation, where the animals cannot be cured and whose afflictions involve permanent and serious disability. The position has recently been well stated by the Australian RSPCA, in terms of the methods used and the skills required of those involved.

Methods   The method of killing will vary according to species and circumstances. All methods must, however, satisfy the same basic criteria:

- death without panic, pain or distress;
- instant death or unconsciousness;
- reliability for both single or large numbers;
- simplicity and minimal maintenance;
- minimal environmental impact;
- minimal emotional impact on operators or observers.

Skill

The skill of operators is vital for the humane killing of animals and they must have appropriate training in:

- animal handling;
- selection of best killing method;
- application of killing method;
- maintenance of equipment.

Methods for killing animals in unplanned, emergency situations will depend upon a number of factors including:

- availability of help, particularly trained or experienced help;
- suitability of equipment available;
- the perceived condition of the animal.

If an animal is seriously injured and is suffering and there is no alternative other than for it to be killed, it must be done expeditiously by the most appropriate means available. If, however, there is the opportunity to obtain expert assistance and/or the suffering is minimal and can be endured, the animal must be made as comfortable as possible until assistance arrives.

Legislation

EU law sets rules to protect the welfare of livestock at slaughter, including prior stunning, but provides exemptions for 'religious' slaughter. In the UK, the conditions under which 'religious' slaughter without stunning is allowed to take place are laid down, but enforcement of the law on a Member State's territory is the responsibility of that State.

Gregory and Lowe (1999) carried out a survey of slaughtering requirements in 27 countries (53 were contacted). Twenty-six of the countries required stunning before slaughter, but 21 of these made exceptions for 'religious' slaughter, 16 of which laid down separate humane requirements for this. Twenty-six specified the equipment to be used and 22 required that slaughter personnel be specially trained.

However, under the Treaty of Rome, it is not permissible to prohibit the export of livestock to another Member State because of the way it might be treated once there. In 1988, MAFF tried to discourage farmers from exporting sheep for slaughter at the Eid-el Kebir festival in France, but such exports could not be banned.

In 1985, FAWC recommended that all farm livestock should be stunned before slaughter and this was accepted by government, but exemptions were made for so-called 'religious' slaughter by Jews and Muslims (see Box 4.5).

In some parts of the world, the use of a stunner could transform the situation. For example, WSPA campaigned in 1994 to introduce the captive bolt stunner to developing countries such as Uganda and Zaire, where, quite apart from long journeys to the slaughterhouse, cattle have their throats cut in a very painful manner. A typical slaughterhouse may handle 30,000 animals a year and one captive bolt stunner could be used for up to ten times this number. This is a good example of a practicable way of eliminating a vast amount of suffering very quickly, although there are also concerns about the unlicensed use of such stunners.

Box 4.5 *'Religious' Slaughter*

In 1985 when FAWC recommended that all animals slaughtered by 'religious' methods should be reviewed by the communities concerned so as to develop alternatives which permit stunning, nearly all European countries provided exemptions from stunning in their legislation for Jewish and Muslim slaughter.

UK legislation required that animals slaughtered in a slaughter-house should be stunned before slaughter unless slaughter was carried out by means of a 'mechanically operated instrument in proper repair'. But exemption was given for Jewish (Shechita), Muslim (Halal) and Sikh (Jhakta) methods, which involve cutting the throat with a knife or decapitation (for Jhakta), all without stunning. There may be conditions laid down as to the sharpness of the knife and the qualifications and training of the operator: these are generally most strict in the case of Shechita (Levinger, 1995), in which religious principles 'make it impossible to stun the animal previous to slaughter'.

These are complex matters and it is easy but unhelpful to oversimplify the issues involved. Whatever the method of slaughter, much depends upon the skill and commitment of the operator, the scale of the operation and the extent of supervision and control. Unsatisfactory episodes occur in all methods and it should not be assumed that, whatever the method, those involved do not care about the welfare of the animal. Part of the problem is that religious principles are not susceptible to scientific reasoning and very strong feelings are held on all sides.

Improvements have been made, especially in the restraining pens used to hold animals during slaughter, which necessarily vary with the size and species of the animal. The important thing is to find better ways of minimizing the stress and suffering of all animals before and during slaughter.

The principle of stunning seems right, but this still leaves open the method of stunning, the subsequent method of slaughter and, very importantly, the interval between the two. Done properly, it may be regarded as satisfactory, and this is also argued for methods of 'religious' slaughter. But where the scale is very large, there are worries about the speed at which the process has to be carried out and, on a small scale, there are worries about lack of supervision.

There may be better ways of doing all these things and they are continually being investigated. Gassing seems attractive, but the right mixture of gases (eg CO_2 and argon) may be difficult to achieve in practice. For example, about 50 million male chicks are disposed of annually in Britain by being dropped into a container filled with more than 99 per cent CO_2. This poses practical problems, but CO_2 is probably not even the best gas to use. Mixtures of CO_2 and argon appear better, but the residual level of oxygen is critical: it has to be less than two per cent.

Currently, pigs in Denmark are gathered by machines and quietly moved into a gas container for slaughter. However, the best methods of killing an animal vary markedly with the species, and research may prompt changes in established practice. For example, the gassing of unwanted (male) day-old chicks now seems less satisfactory and other methods are being developed.

Mutilations

Some mutilations are carried out on a very large scale in the UK and worldwide. The reasons vary from the purely cosmetic, as in the case of tail docking of puppies in the UK, to human and animal safety such as the castration of male cattle, but many are actually related to maintaining good animal welfare such as the beak-trimming of hens to prevent cannibalism. The major mutilations for different kinds of animals are given in Table 4.3.

FAWC is against all mutilations of farm animals but recognizes that some are required within current production systems, in order to avoid even worse welfare problems. However, the nose-ringing of pigs, for example, is aimed at better *pasture* management, not that of the pig. The insertion of a nose-ring is intended to prevent rooting in the soil and is effective in reducing damage to pasture, but it also limits nest-building, the digging of wallows and the extraction of stones for chewing. This creates frustration and reduces the pig's welfare. Thus mutilations not only represent welfare concerns because of the action itself but also because of its consequent effects on behaviour of importance to the animal. Beak-trimming in poultry, for example, restricts the preening of feathers, which is an important aspect of chicken behaviour and contributes to physical well-being.

Table 4.3 *The Main Mutilations*

Mutilation	Species affected
Tail docking	Pigs, dogs, dairy cows (in New Zealand), horses
Beak-trimming	Poultry
Castration and spaying	Cattle, sheep, pigs, dogs, cats
De-clawing	Cats, turkeys
Dehorning	Cattle
Ear-punching (for identification)	Cattle, sheep
Ear-cropping	Dogs
Nose-ringing	Pigs (outdoor), bulls, boars, bears
Debarking	Dogs
Branding	Cattle, horses
Dubbing	Turkeys, cockerels

In general, the RSPCA takes the same view, opposing 'unnecessary' mutilations. However, the RSPCA advocates the neutering of domestic cats and dogs as early as possible, thus preventing unwanted breeding and the creation of strays (see later).

Examples of welfare problems have been used throughout this chapter mainly to illustrate the arguments deployed. But the total list of welfare issues for all classes of animal is very extensive.

Companion Animals

The numbers of companion animals (see Table 4.4) have to be considered (as with agricultural animals) in relation to their size, and there is very great variation between species and, indeed, within some species (eg dogs).

In Australia, 66 per cent of households have pets: 43 per cent with dogs, 29 per cent cats, 19 per cent birds and 15 per cent fish. New Zealand statistics are remarkably similar.

Fewer stray dogs are now having to be rescued in Britain. In 1987, the RSPCA rescued nearly 120,000: in 1995 it was down to 40,000. In the same period, strays taken in by the Battersea Dogs Home (BDH) fell from 25,000 to fewer than 10,000. However, the National Canine Defence League found a 13 per cent increase in

Table 4.4 *Numbers of Companion Animals in the UK*

Type of Animal	Number (millions)
Horses and ponies	0.90
Dogs	6.65
Cats	7.18
Caged birds	1.60
Other pets small mammals	2.70
Ornamental fish	24.38

the number of stray dogs rounded up from 1 April 1996 to 31 March 1997. Of the total of 106,000, 17,000 were destroyed.

Stray cats increase by tens of thousands annually, as unwanted kittens are thrown on to the streets. It has been estimated that some 50 million cats are abandoned annually in the USA.

Unwanted dogs and cats are rehoused by the Blue Cross, the National Canine Defence League and Cats Protection, with great care to match the animal to the new home. The Wood Green Animal Shelter takes in some 7000 unwanted dogs a year and the National Canine Defence League cared for 11,000 dogs in 1997.

The Problem of Strays

Stray dogs and cats are a global problem, but the problem may not be exactly the same in different parts of the world and one needs to ask where the strays come from: it may not always be mainly from the breeding of strays – certainly it cannot have been so initially. In India, Thailand, Australia, many states in Central America and many in Southern Europe, the problem is, specifically, stray dogs; it has been estimated that there are two million stray dogs in Taiwan alone. In the countries of Northern Europe there are estimated to be hundreds of thousands of stray cats.

There is often a reluctance to destroy stray animals and surgical sterilization of females is carried out, but this is time-consuming, expensive and not very effective because of the small numbers operated on. If a non-surgical method of sterilization could be developed, it might be usable on a large scale. For both dogs and cats, the answer is to neuter those kept as pets.

Progress is being made in many parts of the world, but much remains to be done. An example of the problems, and some progress, is given by the 'dog recycling plant' (the 'budka') in Kiev that has just been closed, following a campaign by WSPA and Kiev SOS. The budka impounded and processed more than 20,000 dogs and cats each year for fur hats and pet food. But the same system still operates elsewhere. For example, in the Ukrainian city of Odessa over 14,000 dogs and 8000 cats are caught and killed each year under local authority quotas. In Bulgaria, stray dogs are killed by clubbing, shooting and poisoning.

In Japan in 1997, for example, 307,000 cats and 235,000 dogs were destroyed. The conditions under which cats and dogs are kept whilst waiting to be put down are reported to be less than satisfactory.

A major welfare concern, with dogs particularly, is the production of young animals for sale, bred in uncontrolled and often horrifying conditions. So-called 'puppy farming' is probably the most worrying in the UK (see Box 4.6).

Box 4.6 *Puppy Farming*

This is not really farming at all but involves the keeping of dogs to breed puppies for sale and, in the UK, often happens on isolated farms without use of the land. Very often in cramped, cold and filthy conditions, pedigree puppies are raised in their thousands for financial gain.

Bitches are encouraged to breed as frequently as possible, often twice a year, and when they have outlived their usefulness they are simply disposed of. Under the UK Breeding of Dogs Act (1973) anyone keeping more than two breeding bitches and wishing to sell the progeny commercially should be licensed, but many are not. It is usually extremely difficult to secure convictions, since there is no right of entry to unlicensed breeders' properties and evidence is hard to collect.

Puppy farms are common in Asia, often using pedigree dogs imported from the UK in large numbers. There are no complete records of these and those exporting their dogs have no conception of the appalling conditions in which they will be kept. The solution really lies with the public, who should not buy puppies from other than reputable sources. Ideally, the purchaser should see the conditions under which the puppies are produced.

One of the difficulties with pets is that there are few records about the numbers or the ways in which they are kept. With few exceptions (mainly dogs), no licence is required to keep a pet and whilst advice on how to do so is on offer from many organizations (see Table 6.6), no one is obliged to take it. So we can be concerned about the dimensions of a battery cage, but we know little of the cages, or other containers, in which most pets are kept: do we therefore have no basis for concern? The same ignorance applies to the feeding, watering, exercise and many aspects of the welfare of such animals. If regulations are applied to the keeping of farm livestock, why are they not needed for other animals kept by man for pleasure or profit?

Captive Animals

Again there is a problem with size, since totals may be inflated by large numbers of very small animals that may raise few welfare problems. The numbers of animals kept in zoos and circuses are listed in Table 4.5.

Table 4.5 *Zoos and Circuses*

Estimated numbers of world zoos and animals kept	
Total number of zoos	10,000
Estimated number of animals in zoos	5,000,000
'Core' zoos	1200
Number of vertebrate species in 'core' zoos	3000
Total number of vertebrates held in 'core' zoos	1,000,000

Circuses (see also Chapter 5)
305 performing animals in 23 animal circuses in the UK in 1997 (about half being horses and ponies)
85 animals supplied to circuses overseas

Note: Figures for the whole world are not available for circuses. 'Core' zoos are defined as being members of recognized federations or associations.

The welfare problems in zoos are physical, especially with regard to space and provision of secluded areas, social (adequate environment and social group), and psychological, resulting from physical and social problems. The psychological difficulties manifest themselves in, for example compulsive pacing and stereotypies, environ-mental vandalism, hyperaggression, self-mutilation, chronic apathy and perversion of appetite.

Relatively small numbers of animals are kept in UK circuses and the scale of welfare problems, based on the recent Report by Creamer and Phillips (1998), is indicated in Chapter 5.

For zoo animals, the implications are that even well-run zoos nonetheless involve some adverse welfare, almost by definition, because of constraints on space and environmental stimulus. Across the world there are well-documented cases of appalling cruelty, mainly due to lack of care and resources, particularly in regions affected by war. In these cases, animals may be ill-fed, diseased and injured – and left without veterinary treatment. Of the estimated 10,000 zoos in the world, only one in 20 registers its animals: the total number of animals may be as many as five million.

Working Animals

In the UK, the numbers of working animals are small and dominated by horses (a total of about 8000) and dogs: in general, such animals are well cared for.

Worldwide, however, the numbers are very large and animals are used for transport, traction, raising water and threshing grain. For example, in Africa between 10 and 17 million draft animals are employed (Starkey, 1995), 90 per cent of them for primary soil cultivation. In West Africa, about one million draft cattle and 800,000 donkeys and horses are used for work. In South Africa, animal power is mainly important in rural smallholder farming systems. Oxen are the main draft animals and it is estimated that over 500,000 draft oxen are used each year: about 150,000 donkeys are employed. Mules, hinnies and zebra are only used in very small numbers.

Nutrition may be poor in these systems, especially at certain times of the year, but donkeys are frequently overworked, hobbled tightly and turned loose at night to fend for themselves, resulting in poor nutrition, large parasite burdens and body sores. Farriery has little tradition and donkeys' feet usually take care of themselves: welfare problems have been reported where they are used on roads.

In India, home to most of the estimated 35,000 Asian elephants, the world's largest and oldest elephant market is held annually in the northern state of Bihar. Many of the animals are reported to be drugged, are under-nourished and show signs of abnormal behaviour. Normally, it is reported, elephants spend half their time chained to a tree, using leg chains with sharp spikes. Twenty elephants are said to lose their lives each year due to torture and mistreatment in Kerala alone. Most of these elephants are kept for prestige and ivory, however, rather than work.

Animals Used in Sport and Entertainment

Other than those used in zoos and circuses, the animals in this category are mainly horses, dogs and pigeons.

The complexity of the current position in the UK can be illustrated by two estimates:

1   The 378 registered hunts and unregistered packs in Britain kill approximately 20,000 foxes, hares, deer and mink, annually.
2   By comparison, the cats in Britain (6.5 million) have been estimated to kill at least 70 million small mammals and birds annually (Wilkins, 1992). Fox and Macdonald (1997) put the figures much higher (nine million cats; 88 million birds and 164 million mammals), and concluded that cats were probably responsible for 82 per cent of all wildlife kills. With ferrets accounting for 0.003 per cent, gaze hounds[1] accounted for 0.163 per cent, scent hounds[2] for 0.007 per cent, rifles for 0.975 per cent and shotguns for seven per cent.

But these welfare issues really relate to wild animals (see below): the welfare problems of the horses, dogs and other animals used for sport are not well documented. In the world as a whole, there are serious welfare problems with dancing bears, performing monkeys, bull-fighting, baiting of animals and dog fighting. Even the showing

---

1 Gaze hounds such as greyhounds, salukis, lurchers and whippets hunt by sight and kill in a sprint. Prey are mainly hares and rabbits, hunted singly or in pairs.
2 Scent hounds such as foxhounds, staghounds, harriers and beagles hunt by scent, usually in a pack. Mainly, they hunt foxes, red deer, brown hares and mink.

of animals may involve acute welfare problems. For example, show horses may suffer appalling cruelty, in both training and performance. A WSPA investigation in 1993 found a terrible catalogue of cruel methods in South America, inflicted on *Paso Fino* show horses. These included inserting a 15 cm metal pin into the tail to prevent movement; tying heavy chains to the legs to make them lift them higher; inserting chilli peppers into the anus to promote a lively trot; using spiked bits and trimming hooves so sharply that they were painful to walk on.

Wild Animals

Little is known about the wild animals affected by man, and the numbers are hard to estimate, but some information is available for hunting, shooting and fishing.

In the UK, for example, the estimates of the numbers of red deer killed vary from 100 to 1000, red grouse and partridge from 10,000 to 100,000, hares from 5000 to 30,000, foxes from 20,000 to 150,000 and pheasants up to 10 million. The numbers of rabbits, rats and wood pigeons are estimated at up to 10 million whilst the total number of garden birds killed may be as high as 100 million (Fox and Macdonald, 1997). (In the case of wood pigeons the purpose of shooting may be pest control; in the case of garden birds the majority are killed by cats kept as pets.)

In some parts of the world hunting may take forms unfamiliar to most of us. For example, bears are also hunted with dogs. 'Hounding' involves using dogs fitted with radio-collars, which chase a bear until it climbs a tree, from which it is shot down to be mauled by the dogs as it dies: the radio-collar allows the dogs to be located. This is separate from 'spring hunting', which involves waiting for bears to emerge from hibernation, with their cubs, to be shot by trophy hunters. Quite apart from the killing of wild animals for sport or pest control, there may also be a need for population control in the interests of conservation of habitat or animal health. The following are examples of actual cases:

1   In 1993, it was reported that the Yukon Government had embarked on a wolf control programme in order to boost the dwindling caribou populations in the area.

2   Grey squirrels in the UK cause considerable damage to trees, mainly by stripping bark, and foresters argue that populations need to be controlled. In addition, it is thought that they displace the indigenous red squirrel.

3   In Africa's game reserves, elephants are now increasing beyond the capacity of the environment to support them. In the reserves of Zimbabwe and South Africa, annual culls are now routine. Methods are being sought to control their fertility. The future of the elephant is now covered by the UK Elephant Group (UKEG), a consortium of 12 conservation charities.

4   In 1988, it was reported that 800 elk had been relocated by the California Department of Fish and Game in an attempt to solve a local overpopulation problem.

5   In the 1920s, 18 koalas were introduced to Kangaroo Island, South Australia, and by 1997 the numbers were estimated to be about 5000, resulting in severe over-browsing of their preferred food trees (Laslett, 1997). This, it is felt, will lead to tree loss, environmental degradation and koala starvation. A programme has therefore been launched to relocate, rather than cull, 800 sterilized koalas to the south-east of South Australia.

6   The feral Kaimanawa horses in the central part of the North Island of New Zealand have been degrading and destroying important natural tussock-land ecosystems, and shooting from helicopters has been used to reduce the population. This was judged to be more humane than other control methods, but many horse lovers did not agree: as a result, ground shooting was adopted. Since 1997, however, animals are mustered for sale, with buyers completing an adoption form and being screened by the Royal New Zealand Society for the Prevention of Cruelty to Animals (RNZSPCA).

Once again, it is wise to remember that whatever our attitudes to the *reasons* for these activities, be they for human pleasure, profit or to satisfy groundless beliefs, it matters little to the animal.

Whaling

Whales are hunted for profit but many people feel that these large sensitive mammals have a right to be left alone. This feeling, however, does not appear to be generated in relation to the fish which inhabit the same seas.

Those most closely involved with whaling make a distinction between hunting that involves a chase, as in fox and deer hunts, and whaling which it is claimed involves following the animal or predicting where it is going to appear next. The stress, it is argued, is different. Certainly chasing must be a different matter for animals that move in the sea or the air. It can be argued that very rarely can a diving whale or a flying bird be chased by people, and that *chasing* is generally only completely possible on land. Another problem is that it is not possible to distinguish pregnant and suckling females.

But it is not only hunted whales that present welfare problems. Mass strandings also occur and, whether or not this is due to man-made pollution, decisions have to be made about whether to attempt rescue or whether to put them down. Stranding of such large animals presents unique problems, both practical and philosophical. It may be quite impossible to move them at all as they may weigh up to 180 tonnes. Some argue that stranding occurs naturally and the animals should be left to die naturally: others argue that they should be 'put out of their misery'. Part of the problem is to know if they are, in fact, 'in misery'. The question, as always, must be 'are they suffering?' The philosophical difficulty is that clearly their welfare is adversely affected, but so is that of any animal dying naturally. Nevertheless, we do not search the country for animals dying naturally so that we can 'put them out of their misery'. However, we might take a different view if we were sure that the whales were, for example, in pain and certain to die anyway. So, it seems that there are degrees of untreatable suffering where we might judge euthanasia to be the right action. This view is held by many in relation to humans as well.

There is something about very large animals, especially mammals, that affects most of us: their majestic bearing has something to do with it, but it is hard to see the logical force of the distinctions we make. Big cats, elephants and stags have a similar effect, but whales also strike us as particularly harmless and inoffensive.

In countries where whaling has always been an accepted way of obtaining meat, oil and whalebone, attitudes are different and, apart from conservation arguments, it is hard to see why whaling is wrong and fishing is all right. One difference, however, is the sheer difficulty of killing a whale humanely. Stunning is not really possible since, for electrical stunning, electrodes would have to be accurately placed on to the cranium and a sufficient current applied. Similarly, explosive harpoons would have to be placed very accurately, and without such accuracy both methods can cause extreme suffering.

A review of Norwegian whalers (Kestin, 1995) in the period 1992–93 recorded that the use of a grenade-headed harpoon killed about half the whales within 10 seconds: over 90 per cent were dead within 10 minutes but a few survived for up to 50 minutes.

The International Whaling Commission (IWC) was set up in 1946 and has been mainly concerned with conservation, but there has been no general agreement to include the smaller species, dolphins and porpoises. In fact, legislation and agreements on the conservation of whales go back a long way. In 1934, the UK banned the taking of Baleen Whales in coastal waters and the taking of Right Whales outside UK coastal waters.

Worldwide protection was agreed for Right Whales in 1935, for Gray Whales in 1937, for Humpback Whales in 1966, Blue Whales in 1967 and the 1982 meeting of the IWC agreed to a worldwide moratorium for Fin, Sei, Bryde's and Minke Whales. However, some whales are still killed for research purposes.

Animals Used in Experiments

The numbers of animals used in experiments in the UK are known and recorded, since a Home Office licence is required to carry out each experiment and the numbers have to be approved in all cases (see Table 4.6).

In 1996 11,221 procedures were carried out by the UK Defence Evaluation and Research Agency on animals, including marmosets, pigs, rabbits, rhesus monkeys, sheep, goats, guinea pigs, rats and mice: in 1992, the figure was 4500. These figures are higher than those used in cosmetics testing: comparable figures are 3082 animals used, down to 1266 in 1998. In 1997, more than 600,000 animals (mostly mice) were used in other toxicity tests.

In Australia, a survey in 1998 showed that over three million animals were used in one year for the five states that publish figures: of these over two million were fish. Excluding fish, the total was 1,140,641. In New Zealand, the total for 1996 was 264,000, of which 17,000 were fish.

Table 4.6 *Numbers of Animals Used for Experiments in the UK in 1992*

Birds	220,312
Cats	3692
Dogs	9085
Fish	138,251
Mice	1,448,960
Other mammals	137,100
Primates	5018
Rabbits	79,450
Rats	833,004
Reptiles/Amphibians	18,955
Ruminants	34,431
Total	**2,928,258**

Source: HMSO, 1993

Summary

1 The number of animals worldwide is huge, especially in agriculture, those used for sport and hunting, those kept as pets and resulting strays, and those used in experiments.
2 The nature of the problem is that many of these animals do not live or die in welfare-friendly conditions. Ill-treatment and mutilations are common and the totality of suffering is unacceptable.
3 The numbers involved increase the scale of the problem but, to the suffering animal, it is irrelevant whether or not it is just one of many.
4 Furthermore, the suffering animal is not in the least concerned with why it is suffering. Avoidable or unnecessary suffering cannot be justified.

5

The Need for Standards

'Barbarism is the absence of standards to which appeal can be made' (José Ortega Garret)

As mentioned in Chapter 1, there is nothing to be gained by simply bandying about our opinions of animal welfare, each of us using 'welfare' to mean whatever suits our purposes. There has to be an agreed definition of welfare (see Chapter 2), and what represents good welfare has to be spelt out in great detail, for every kind of animal in terms of sex, age and weight, for example, and for a range of situations such as whether the animal has to be housed or kept out-of-doors.

It must be obvious that what is good for a poodle may not be good for a Great Dane; a muddy wallow may suit a pig but a hen requires a dry dust bath. FAWC has attempted to categorize the requirements for the main farm animals and a study of each type of animal characteristically generates a sizeable report to cover its welfare needs. Furthermore these needs cannot be associated with a named system, such as 'free-range' or 'grazing'. An 'outdoor' pig system may be fine on light soils in the summer and totally unsatisfactory on heavy soils in the winter. All outdoor systems are different from a welfare point of view, depending on location, soils, and seasons for example. Any system will be greatly affected by whether the people involved are adequately trained and motivated; whether they are kindly, callous, impatient or tired, and whether they are knowledgeable about the animals they care for and have time to do their jobs properly. So we cannot simply say 'outdoor' systems are good, 'indoor' systems are bad, and this applies to such commonly used terms as 'free-range', 'aviary', 'barn', 'feedlot', 'intensive' and 'extensive'.

There is therefore no possibility of classifying systems as 'welfare-friendly' unless they satisfy all the criteria specified for the animals involved. It is these criteria that have to be decided upon. The 'Five Freedoms' developed by FAWC provide a framework of principles, but they have to be translated into detailed specifications for each animal type.

There are some systems that some people regard as so fundamentally inadequate or wrong (eg battery hen production) that they can be described as 'bad' from a welfare point of view. A system can only be described as 'good' if it satisfies all the relevant criteria but, even then, it could be badly operated. It is these criteria that collectively form welfare standards.

Welfare Standards

Welfare standards depend upon being able to answer such questions as:

- How much space does a hen require?
- How many times a day should a rabbit be fed?
- Is it right to keep a gerbil on its own?
- Does a goldfish need company and a structured environment?
- What is the most humane way to kill a frog?
- Should female cats be spayed?
- What height is it reasonable to ask a horse to jump?
- Should a captive tiger be allowed to hunt live prey?
- Is it permissible to use animals in adverts?
- Should every animal have natural daylight and darkness?
- Should animals be tethered?

It is quite easy to formulate hundreds of such questions and all could be repeated for each species and for different sexes and sizes within each species.

The detail required to answer all these questions is enormous and it may not be easy to agree on the answers. Indeed, very often, the information is not known. There is then a problem of how to obtain the information, for several reasons.

The Cost of Information

However obtained, information may be quite costly, and who is going to pay? In the case of fur-farming, which is not now a very large-scale activity in the UK, FAWC found that it did not know whether the methods used caused poor welfare, although confinement of mink in cages seemed unlikely to satisfy the needs of a wide-ranging predator which swims frequently. However, it judged that the expenditure of public funds could not be justified to find out what conditions would be satisfactory from a welfare point of view. It therefore concluded that the fur-farming industry itself should fund the necessary research, and so far this has not been done in the UK.

The Need for Research

Research may be needed to learn about what matters to an animal. A great deal of work has now been done to establish how much a feature matters, as for example a nest box to a laying hen. This is done by measuring how hard the animal will work or what obstacles it will overcome to gain access to the feature. This is helpful in learning from the animal itself what is important to it and not prejudging the issue from our point of view. This may often produce results that surprise us. However, a simple preference test may not indicate importance at all. Rats and dogs, just like people, may select chocolates in a preference test but that does not mean that these are nutritionally important.

The Assessment of Suffering

It may not be known whether a given practice causes suffering or not: quite often we will not want the relevant experiment to be carried out. How can such an experiment be carried out without causing the very suffering we suspect? If we see a baby being struck a blow, we do not react by saying 'we must carry out research to see if this actually causes suffering', even less do we then say 'how are we going to measure this suffering scientifically?' But the fact that it is easy to find parallels in animals should not blind us to the fact that we do not always agree on the obvious answer. Take hunting, for example. There are radically different views, all strongly held, as to whether a fox or a deer suffers when hunted. Furthermore, we will not all agree about how this should be assessed. Sometimes we really only want our personal beliefs or prejudices confirmed, and sometimes we really would rather not know.

Information on Large-scale Operations

Sometimes we lack knowledge about very large-scale operations (eg birds in broiler houses, abattoirs, importation of pets and laboratory experiments) and monitoring and observation are difficult to arrange. There are examples of large-scale operations in agriculture where new knowledge needs to be obtained under practical conditions. This can only be done with the cooperation of the relevant part of industry, but for the results to be credible, experimental procedures have to be independently devised and monitored. This arrangement has been successfully carried out by FAWC in cooperation with, for example, the poultry industry. One advantage is that the results are seen to be relevant to the industry and are therefore more acceptable. Also the practicalities and costs of improvements can be assessed under practical conditions. Such costs are often not as high as feared and it is important to establish this (see Chapter 7).

A quite different example is that of shooting an individual animal in a herd under field conditions. It is usually assumed that domesticated animals are best killed away from their fellows but, in some cases, such as deer, it appears that the stress of capturing and confining an animal is greater than that of a clean shot in the field, and that nearby animals appear to remain unconcerned. This also seems to be the case with natural predation with lion attacks on wildebeeste for example. The unharmed animals rapidly resume normal behaviour, such as grazing. Indeed, this killing in the presence of what are termed 'conspecifics' may well be acceptable for some farm animals.

The danger of generalizing about such topics is illustrated by mink, where the odour given off by scent glands during skinning may be much more upsettting to other mink than the actual death of one of their number.

The Interpretation of Observations

If we depend on observation, how will we agree on interpretation? All these exceptions and anomalies show how careful we have to be in simply relying on our observations and what we think of as common-sense interpretations of what we see.

Many cases of cruelty and poor welfare are so obvious that no further investigation is required or desired by anyone. There are also many cases, however, where it is not obvious, or where we simply do not know whether the animal is suffering (or how much) or where we disagree about the answer. This last point may even apply to examples where some think the issue is absolutely obvious that suffering occurs whilst others hold the view, just as strongly, that it is obvious that no suffering is involved, or no more than is natural or acceptable.

Such disagreements illustrate the need for evidence, objectively and independently obtained and assessed. Not all scientific evidence will be accepted as meeting these needs, for four main reasons:

1   Scientists often disagree, so opposing scientific evidence can be found.
2   Science does not deal in absolute knowledge; it uses hypotheses, theories and laws for as long as they are not refuted.
3   Not all scientists are unbiased or wholly independent.
4   There are some concepts including 'suffering' that may not be susceptible to scientific 'proof'. In any case, scientific experimentation has difficulty in proving negatives.

Furthermore, the question may not be 'does suffering occur?' but 'does it matter?' This will depend on the degree of suffering. We all suffer and there is much unavoidable suffering including the ways in which wild animals behave in their natural environment. Not only do predators catch, kill and eat their prey (and not necessarily in that order) but males fight for territory and females. In the second case, the risk of severe injury and consequent suffering is real.

In trying to judge issues of suffering, we need all the help we can get, including scientific evidence. Emotion is usually involved in generating concern and may be a good guide as to whether action is needed: science may be needed to decide exactly what to do about it, but can also help in judging whether action is justified at all.

The main roles of science may then be summarized as follows:

1   To measure and assess the effect of something (an action, a set of conditions, a deprivation or a constraint) on the animal's physical, physiological and mental state and responses; this is important in answering the question 'what does this do to the animal?'
2   To measure and assess the relative importance of something (a feature, a set of conditions or a facility and the avoidance of any of these) to the individual or group of animals. This helps to answer the question 'how much does it matter to the animal?'

So science can suggest the best way of solving a problem from a welfare point of view but not necessarily from an economic point of view, and then devise ways of testing the success of the solution. It is important, of course, that such tests do not themselves adversely affect welfare. The fact is that standards have to deal objectively with all these and many other questions, and have to be based on what is known as opposed to subjective opinion. They therefore have to be set by an independent authoritative body, able to draw upon scientific evidence and relevant practical experience.

Standards for Farm Livestock

FAWC attempts to set standards for farm animals in Britain and there are similar bodies, often modelled on FAWC, in other countries. In New Zealand, for example, two bodies operate, a Farm Animal Welfare Advisory Committee (FAWAC) and a National Animal Ethics Advisory Committee (see Chapter 6). The recommendations of such bodies form the basis of welfare standards now being imposed on livestock producers by big retailers and by quality assurance schemes (see Chapter 7). The species covered include not only the main farm livestock but also, for example, ostrich and emu in New Zealand (AWAC, 1998). In the USA in 1999 the Federation of Animal Science Societies (FASS) completed the first revised edition of the Guide for the Care and Use of Agricultural Animals in Agricultural Research and Teaching.

But farm animals are only one group and there is a need for comparable standard-setting bodies for other groups.

Standards for Companion Animals

In the UK, a Companion Animal Welfare Council (CAWC) was established in 1999, organized along similar lines to FAWC but without government funding, but it will take some time to cover even the most common companion animals. FAWC has been operating for nearly 20 years and was preceded by a Farm Animal Welfare Advisory Committee.

In many other European countries, relevant welfare councils cover almost all animals (see Table 6.1).

Standards for Zoo Animals

For captive animals, other than farm animals and pets, a major issue is the control of zoos. Over recent years, the role of zoos has changed, from being solely concerned with entertainment to a major concern with education and conservation.

However, a report by the WSPA and the Born Free Foundation (BFF) considered that most zoos were still predominantly concerned with human recreation, that present zoo-based conservation strategy would have only a marginal impact on species conservation and that the educational value of zoos was very limited (WSPA/BFF, 1994).

Greater opportunities for travel and natural history programmes on television now fulfil many of the original purposes of zoos and the report concluded that most zoo animals face a life in captivity in which their welfare is severely compromised (see Box 5.1).

Box 5.1 *Zoochosis*

A zoochotic animal, defined by Bill Travers of Zoo Check (Travers, 1993), is one that is 'mentally damaged by captivity'. Such animals exhibit 'stereotypies' or obsessive, abnormal, repetitive behaviour. This is often seen in zoo animals and circuses and is also observed in stabled horses mainly due to environmental deprivation.

Webster (1994) divides stereotypies into 'movement' and 'oral' types. Examples of the former are 'weaving', for example by horses and polar bears, 'pacing' by carnivores such as polar bears and big cats, 'looping' for example by mink, voles and chipmunks, and 'rocking' by primates, including man. Oral stereotypies include 'bar-chewing' by pigs and cattle, 'crib-biting and windsucking' by horses, 'tongue rolling' by cattle, especially veal calves, and 'thumb-sucking' by primates, including man.

Such behaviour is commonly seen in zoos and in the Zoo Check Report on zoochosis, following visits to over 100 zoos in the UK, Europe, the Far East and North America, many examples were recorded on film. This report identified the causes as separation from natural habitat, enforced idleness, direct control by humans, absence of social life, use of drugs in fertility control, and caging with all its alien features of artificial diet, lighting, noises, proximity to alien species and human visitors.

In addition to the stereotypies mentioned, zoo animals have exhibited over-grooming, vomiting in gorillas, coprophagia and self-mutilation. The contention is that, in extreme cases, these animals are being driven insane.

On the positive side, there is now a World Zoo Conservation Strategy and some zoological federations (notably the American Zoo and Aquarium Association) have established voluntary minimal welfare standards (see Box 5.2).

Box 5.2 *World Zoo Conservation Strategy (WZCS)*

The International Union of Directors of Zoological Gardens (IUDZG) published the World Zoo Conservation Strategy in 1993. This sets out the structure and agenda for future zoos, with conservation at the heart of the zoos' role. Its objectives are to support actively coordinated programmes for the conservation of endangered species (*in situ* and *ex situ*) and their habitats, to support increasing scientific knowledge for the benefit of conservation, and to promote public and political awareness of the need for conservation. Currently the space in the 'best' zoos devoted to endangered species is estimated at five to ten per cent of the total, breeding 1–200 endangered species out of a total of nearly 6000. So far, successes have been limited (see Stud-books: *International Zoo Yearbook,* volumes 31 and 32).

The UK has a Zoo Licensing Act (1981) but the EU has not yet established comparable legal provision. WSPA and BFF (1994) make ten major recommendations for zoo reform (see Appendix 1). Zoos are generally defined as establishments which possess, or manage collections of, mainly wild animals which are confined for exhibition or study and which are displayed to the public (see IUDZG et al, 1993). However, many zoos regard themselves as centres for captive breeding of rare and endangered species. This raises two major issues: how should such animals be kept and how should they be released into the wild, if breeding is successful? (see Chapter 6). The 'Five Freedoms' are a useful test for captive animals of all kinds but exhibited animals also require some protection of their privacy so that visitors do not intrude adversely; enclosures should not be sterile, leading to unnatural and stereotyped behaviour; animals should not be isolated from their own species (or, indeed, some other species); ventilation with fresh air must be ensured and the needs for animals to be active, including searching for food, must be met.

Standards to be applied under the 1981 Act are currently under review, taking into account appropriate modifications to the Five Freedoms and the need to implement the EU Council Directive Relating to the Keeping of Wild Animals in Zoos (1999). The latter provides for the licensing and inspection of zoos and sets the framework for both conservation activities and standards of animal care.

Standards for Circus Animals

There are circuses (ten in the UK in 1997) that do not involve animals at all, so they cannot be regarded as an essential part of such entertainment. For animals that do appear in circuses, however, there are special problems, some of them associated with the need for the circuses to be mobile. Circuses often move frequently and the animal's accommodation has to be easily transported: this places constraints on size and weight and thus on space allowance. When circuses are stationary, accommodation could be more spacious, but this is apparently not necessarily so, partly for reasons of cost.

Creamer and Phillips (1998) found that, during 1997, 23 animal circuses toured the UK, with a total of 305 performing animals, half of them horses and ponies. Other animals used included camels, dogs, domestic cats, leopards, lions, tigers, sea lions, elephants and a rhinoceros. Eighty-five animals were known to be supplied to circuses overseas and many may travel constantly between continents. Travelling means long hours shut up in cramped transporters and 'beastwagons'.

If there are no Christmas performances, the animals spend several months in winter quarters, often with minimal exercise periods. Legal controls seem to be quite inadequate and circuses are exempt from the Dangerous Wild Animals Act, 1976, the Zoo Licensing Act, 1981 and have exemptions from the Convention on International Trade in Endangered Species (CITES) (see Box 5.3). The Performing Animals (Regulation) Act 1925 and the Performing Animals Rules do not lay down standards of animal welfare or disease control, and the Protection of Animals Act (1911) does not encompass the main areas of suffering in circus animals.

Box 5.3 *The Convention on International Trade in Endangered Species*

CITES has the status of an international treaty, ratified by 120 nations, designed to regulate the trade in endangered species (which are listed in an Appendix to the treaty) between signatory countries.

Zoos and similar organizations believe that it unnecessarily restricts their activities, whereas welfare and environmental organizations in general believe that CITES is less effective than it should be.

CITES is not aimed primarily at animal welfare and, indeed, when enforcing authorities confiscate animals being imported in contravention of the Convention, welfare problems often prevent their return to the country of origin and they may end up in the zoo that was their original destination.

CITES contains certain exemptions for circuses, which allow movements of circus animals without permits or certificates provided that certain details have been registered with the management authority.

Local authorities have great difficulty in controlling circuses since they move on very rapidly and there is little time for inspection and the necessary processing of papers. Creamer and Phillips (1998) recommend that circus animals should come under the Zoo Licensing Act (1981), which could control winter quarters and transport arrangements. Although the number of animals is small in the UK, they include some very long-lived species and ones that, in the wild, range very widely. The numbers involved worldwide are not available.

Kiley-Worthington (1990) found no evidence of cruelty and regarded it as quite unnecessary for training. Creamer and Phillips (1998), however, in a long and thorough undercover investigation found a horrifying catalogue of vicious cruelty, both physical and psychological. The evidence came from over 7000 hours of observation, 400 hours of it on film. Much of the cruelty was by individuals and could not be said to be an inevitable part of circus activity.

However, many would argue that circus life is entirely inappropriate for wild animals and inevitably involves severe deprivation of essential freedoms. A major deprivation is of space, close confinement and tethering being common. In the study by Creamer and Phillips (1998), 96 per cent of the total time, averaged for all animals, was spent in containers. Lions and lionesses, for example, spent 92 to 98 per cent of their time in 'beastwagons'. Much of the cruelty was associated with training, involving, for example, severe beating of tethered elephants with iron bars.

Circuses are probably of rapidly decreasing importance in the UK but this is not so in other countries. In the US, for example, they are considered a significant part of the traditions and culture throughout the country. Many humane societies in the US believe that the use of animals – especially wild animals – should be prohibited, but this is unlikely in the foreseeable future.

Standards for Work Animals

Animals used for work have to be trained as well as used, so standards have to cover both. Many other animals are also trained: cats are 'house-trained' but otherwise tend to be a law unto themselves; pet dogs are trained and can be destructive and dangerous if they are not. If the idea of training seems in any way objectionable, just consider the problems associated with untrained dogs, horses, cats or elephants.

Training

In 1990 UFAW published the proceedings of a symposium under the title of 'Animal Training'. This covered virtually all species and their functions, including the little-known use of Capuchin monkeys to assist severely paralysed individuals to become more independent. These monkeys possess exceptional manual dexterity, form close, affectionate, responsive relationships with humans when raised with them from an early age and can live in captivity for over 30 years. This 'Helping Hands' programme has been operating since 1979, the monkeys having been trained to help high-level quadriplegics perform many small tasks.

The general conclusions of the UFAW Symposium were that:

- most animals appear to enjoy being trained (though the previous section on circuses demonstrates that this depends on the people and the methods);
- training depends upon the animal's cooperation and is best based on the use of rewards;
- negative reinforcement, other than by voice, should only be used where an animal could endanger itself or others (this seems to be comparable to that employed by wild animals such as elephants in training their offspring);
- even the most 'exploited' animals such as guide dogs for the blind appear to gain some reward from their service: good welfare for them depends mainly upon a good environment outside the working time;
- training is best regarded as an art rather than a science;
- trainers should themselves be trained.

Clearly, training standards would be helpful for each of the species involved.

Use of Animals for Work

Clearly, animals being used for work, particularly in transport and traction, may be over-worked, and in many parts of the world undoubtedly are, often to a disgraceful extent.

This was the case for horses in the UK some 100 years ago. It was largely the dreadful conditions and treatment of work-horses, as well as that of dogs, cats, goats and rabbits, all in London, that motivated Maria Dickin in establishing the People's Dispensary for Sick Animals (PDSA) in 1917. Overwork may relate to the duration of the work, the rate of performance (eg speed of movement), the size of the load to be pulled or carried, or the weather conditions or conditions underfoot in which the animal has to operate.

There are often serious deficiencies in the ways in which animals are harnessed. These are sometimes cruel and often very inefficient in not allowing the animal to use its strength properly or actually causing pain and discomfort. The efficient use of work animals in the agriculture of developing countries is an extremely important topic because of the large numbers involved, the degree of suffering and the economic importance of the work they do (see Starkey and Ndiamé, 1986; Starkey, 1995). In addition, nutrition, water supply and rest periods may be inadequate and the physical treatment of the animal may amount to cruel abuse including the use of sticks, whips and goads, especially on sensitive parts of the body.

There are few standards covering any of these issues – and much always depends on human attitudes. Even guide dogs, which are both work and companion animals, need considerate treatment, not only when working but in their 'off' periods.

Standards for Wild Animals

If wild animals are left alone in adequate habitats, there would seem to be little reason for human concern. But a habitat that is ideal for a given species may allow it to reproduce too successfully, sometimes because its main predators, such as wolves in the case of deer, have been eliminated, and it may end up destroying its own environment, including its food supply. The animals may then suffer starvation, parasitism and disease, dying in large numbers at times of stress. There is thus a case for population control (see Chapter 4).

Pest Control

Pest control is a special case of the need for population control. In New Zealand, for example, many of the 25 introduced mammals are now viewed as pests for one of the following five reasons:

1   environmental degradation;
2   endangering native plants and animals;
3   loss of primary production;
4   maintaining livestock disease;
5   damage done to private property and human health.

Possums, feral pigs, feral goats and red deer affect forests, rabbits affect tussock grasslands, hares and possums affect crops; a whole range of animals including feral cats, stoats and rats prey on native animals. Brushtail possums, red deer and ferrets are reservoirs of bovine TB. The case for control is overwhelming, but the problems lie in the welfare implications of the methods used.

Where we interfere with wild animals accidentally, as for example in road accidents, it is possible to provide warning signs and speed limits, but there is no question of setting standards. On the other hand, where interference is deliberate, as in hunting, shooting and fishing, standards or codes of behaviour are desirable.

In the UK, field sports do have codes of behaviour for the protection of the environment and human safety and codes which are specific to the target animal. These may not be judged adequate from the point of view of animal welfare and there are wide differences of opinion about them. Worldwide, the position is less satisfactory, with the hunting and trapping of animals for fur, feathers and animal parts and their sale for pets, laboratory use, zoos, menageries and circuses. Trade in endangered species, however, is controlled by CITES (see Box 5.3).

Standards for Animals Used in Experiments

In Great Britain, anyone carrying out experiments on animals has to have a Home Office Licence and approved experiments may only be carried out at approved establishments. Both procedures and facilities are open to inspection by Home Office Inspectors. The legal basis for this is the Animals (Scientific Procedures) Act of 1986, which replaced the Cruelty to Animals Act of 1876. Many other countries also formulated or revised their laws in the 1970s and 1980s. The Council of Europe Convention for the Protection of Vertebrate Animals used for Experimental and other Scientific Purposes was adopted in May 1985 and came into effect on 1 October 1986.

This legislation now applies to the UK as a whole. The 1986 Act provides for the approval of guidance notes and codes of practice by the Home Secretary. UFAW and other organizations have produced such guidelines. Animals provided for experiments have to come from a 'Home Office approved' breeding establishment. The legislation, however, is directed at procedures (that have to be approved) rather than welfare, although there are requirements that any animal suffering 'severe pain or severe distress which cannot be alleviated' must be killed humanely, by methods which are laid down for each species. Furthermore, there are recognized exceptions, including, for example, any recognized veterinary, agricultural or animal husbandry practices, unless they are performed by novel or experimental methods.

Legislation

The last section illustrated an area which is covered primarily by legislation in the UK and with an Animal Procedures Committee that advises the Home Office on the use of animals in scientific research. Many personal or project licence applications (eg for cosmetics testing) are also referred to the Committee.

It is not possible to summarize the relevant legislation worldwide but the law applying mainly to England and Wales was summarized and reviewed in a book by Cooper (1987) and a 'Summary of Legislation Relative to Animal Welfare at the Levels of the European Economic Community and the Council of Europe' was published by the Eurogroup for Animal Welfare in 1987. Both of these publications include all the classes of animals dealt with in the present book. (See also the Bibliography.)

The Standing Committee of the European Convention for the Protection of Animals is a good example where recommendations for legislation are being steadily developed based on well considered and detailed standards. These have recently been adopted for ducks, geese and their crossbreeds, with a revised version for fur animals, and recommendations for pigs, rabbits and turkeys are being worked on.

In the US, the Animal Welfare Act (AWA) is continually being updated for virtually all species and details can be found in the bulletins produced by the Animal Welfare Information Centre and published by the National Agricultural Library.

Evolution of Standards

Since standards depend upon knowledge, from scientific investigation and from observation and practical experience, they cannot remain unchanged over long periods of time: they need to be updated. Furthermore, society's attitudes change over time and standards ultimately have to reflect how we wish to regulate people's behaviour. Standards thus evolve and the ways in which they are framed have to accommodate this evolutionary process. This is most easily achieved when welfare-oriented innovation is encouraged by those most closely involved.

It is right and sensible that people should be able to say, of any practice that affects animals, 'we do not wish to live in a society which allows that kind of thing'. Such decisions should not be based wholly on emotion, but emotions are legitimately involved. Decisions should preferably not be made in ignorance of relevant information, but this is not always available. So it is possible and, indeed, inevitable that society may wish to ban what are regarded as cruel practices. However, a great deal more knowledge is required to say what should be put in place of the banned practice in cases where something is required.

Battery cages for hens are a current example. Many people wish to ban them and some countries such as Sweden have decided to do so, but few scientists believe that a wholly satisfactory alternative is yet available that can cope with anything like the number of hens in current use. That is one of the reasons why the recent (1999) decision to ban battery cages in the EU does not envisage full implementation until 2013. Another reason is to allow reasonable time for new investment to be absorbed. Alternative intensive systems such as aviaries and free-range systems, however, are not without their welfare problems of, for example, disease and feather pecking.

Designing something better requires a deep understanding of the needs of the laying hen and the determination to meet those needs in ways that can be practically and economically adopted. For this, we need to encourage all those involved to try out improvements so that we can learn how to do it better. FAWC has stated that it finds battery cages unacceptable but cannot yet identify a totally satisfactory alternative that does not also have unacceptable welfare problems.

This reinforces the idea that standards should not prescribe detailed systems that should be carried out but should identify the welfare criteria that should be met. It is quite possible that these can ultimately be met by several different production systems.

The same is true for better zoo design, better cages for rabbits, better methods of breaking-in horses, better ways of training dogs, killing pigs or preventing and curing diseases. The law is essentially prescriptive and mainly against activities, processes or devices.

Standards are to set targets, short-term and long-term, that treatment of animals should aim at or actually achieve. The public then have the power to support or shun those activities and systems that achieve (or fail to achieve) minimum standards. The reasons for distinguishing between short- and long-term aims is to make it possible to insist on the achievement of those goals that are immediately achievable, whilst recognizing that these may fall short of the ideal. Where people are expected to conform to short-term standards, it is only fair to state where these are not the long-term ideals, so that people are not misled into thinking that the immediate changes, which may involve substantial costs, are the end of the road. It is also desirable to encourage people not to rest on the achievement of short-term standards but to make their own contributions in the achievement of the long-term aims.

The underlying theme is to move away from confrontation and enforcing change to cooperation in the improvement of animal welfare by all concerned.

Summary

1   It is essential that what constitutes good welfare for each kind of animal should be defined: this is what is meant by standards.
2   It is highly desirable that such standards should be agreed and accepted very widely and ultimately worldwide.
3   Standards must be based on all relevant and reliable information, from scientific investigation and from practical observation and experience.
4   It is important that better methods of assessing both animal needs and degree of suffering should be continually developed.
5   Standards should be set by independent, authoritative bodies based on wide consultation.

6

Organizations Concerned
with Animal Welfare

*'The greatness of a nation can be judged by the way
we treat our animals'* (Mahatma Gandhi)

The Relevant Organizations

Many of the bodies referred to in this chapter are specialized by
species or activity, whilst others cover a wide range of both. Amongst
the latter are the RSPCA for the UK and WSPA for the world as a
whole. Details of these organizations and their main areas of concern
are given in Appendix 2. The appendix also gives details of the World
Animal Net, the global network for animal protection.

Relevant organizations in the field of animal welfare are difficult
to classify, partly because of overlapping functions, but their purposes
and functions represent ways of considering them. Following the
previous chapter, a useful starting point is provided by the standards
and who sets them.

Bodies that set standards need to be authoritative and independent but are not normally able to set appropriate standards for
all species. The FAW and the FAWAC of New Zealand are examples,
dealing with farm animals only. However, several such as the Belgian,
Danish and Dutch bodies have much wider remits, but their ability
to cover all species may nonetheless be limited by resources. They
may be supported by other bodies attempting to establish the ethical

basis for standards. These, too, may relate to a sector such as the New Zealand National Animal Ethics Advisory Committee (NAEAC) but, if one body can look across all species, it might be expected that it would concentrate on the ethical basis.

Codes of practice are generally guidelines, without legal force, although conformity to them may be used as evidence in cases of alleged cruelty. They, too, are not able to cover all species and, indeed, most codes of practice relate to only one species and how it should be kept.

In some cases, however, as with methods of killing, codes may cover a wide range of species, partly to emphasize that the most appropriate method will vary with the species and with its age and size. Different organizations may therefore produce codes relating to their special remits (eg cats, pets, zoos) and not all will be dis-interested and independent. In the UK, MAFF issues codes of recom-mendations for farm animals based on the advice of FAWC.

Those organizations involved in the horse industry, or in salmon farming, however, may produce codes of practice for their own members. These aim to ensure that all members follow 'best practice' but they do not necessarily address all the welfare issues and may ignore those that concern outsiders but are not perceived as problems within the sector.

Some of the standards and codes may also become law and advisory bodies exist in many countries to recommend what changes are required to improve welfare legislation. Examples of these bodies within Europe are given in Table 6.1.

Monitoring of the extent to which standards, codes and legisla-tion are being followed is often difficult and expensive. In the UK, MAFF veterinarians may monitor practice in agriculture and Home Office inspectors keep an eye on experimental and laboratory animals but no one can monitor the treatment of pets within private house-holds.

Only if cruelty is identified is it possible to pursue offenders and this depends upon it being reported to government agencies, local authorities or welfare organizations. Only some of the latter are able to launch prosecutions, the RSPCA being a notable example. In many cases, problem animals are no longer 'owned' by anyone but have been abandoned, resulting in strays (see Chapter 4): others are aband-oned by their owners because they can no longer be fed and others

Table 6.1 *Advisory Bodies in Europe*

Country	Name	Ministry Responsible
Belgium	The Animal Welfare Council	Agriculture
Denmark	The Ethical Council concerning Animals	Justice
France	No Council but several commissions	Agriculture and Fisheries
Germany	Federal Commission on Animal Welfare	Food, Agriculture and Forestry
The Netherlands	Council on Animal Affairs	Agriculture and Public Health
Norway	Norwegian Council for Animal Ethics	Agriculture
Sweden	Animal Welfare Advisory Committee	Agriculture
UK	Farm Animal Welfare Council	Agriculture, Fisheries and Food

Table 6.2 *Animals in Need of Rescue*

Species	Reason
Dogs	Abandoned as strays when no longer wanted
Donkeys	Too old to work or simply grossly neglected
Horses	Not wanted any longer
Oiled sea-birds	Caused by oil spills
Swans and ducks	Poisoned by lead pellets
Bears	Used for sport or entertainment
Zoo animals	Closure of zoo
Dolphins	Closure of dolphinaria
Badgers and others	Injured in road accidents
Birds	Damaged by collision with power lines, lighthouses etc

are wild animals that have been injured. Examples of these cases are given in Table 6.2, to illustrate the range and scale of the problem.

Other animals may have been ill-treated and have to be removed from the control of the owner, or need to be liberated from inade-

Table 6.3 *UK Charities Engaged in Rescue and Rehabilitation*

Species	Charity
Donkeys	The Donkey Sanctuary
Dogs	Battersea Dogs Home
Cats	Cats Protection
Dogs, cats and others	RSPCA and Wood Green Animal Shelter
Bears	WSPA
Zoo animals	WSPA
Horses and ponies	Essex Horse and Pony Protection Society (EHPPS), Home of Rest for Horses, International League for the Protection of Horses

quate zoos or dolphinaria. All these need rescue and rehabilitation, and many charities exist for this purpose (see Table 6.3).

Wild animals may also need a service of this kind. They include those injured in road accidents and those injured but not destroyed as a consequence of hunting, shooting and fishing, especially dolphins, whales and porpoises unintentionally caught in marine fishing nets. Other wild animals are intentionally trapped or poisoned, because they are considered to be pests, predators on game or spreaders of disease (see Boxes 6.1, 6.2 and 6.3). Others are unintentionally injured by traps, or poisoned by agrochemicals and substantial numbers of swans are affected by lead weights lost in angling.

Box 6.1 *Trapping*

In 1987, the International Organization for Standardization Committee (ISO) was established to develop international standards for humane animal traps. Trapping has a long history and currently over 500,000 people are directly involved in trapping in North America, for example. Attempts to improve the methods used have made slow progress.

The EU agreed in 1991 to abolish the use of the cruel and inhumane leg-hold trap in all 15 member countries by 1995 but it is still widely used elsewhere, although the steel-jawed variety is now used infrequently. There is still no approved standard, but best management practices are being developed – sets of recommendations for specific trapping conditions. Snares are also a source of concern, especially self-locking snares in which the slowly tightening noose is both cruel and indiscriminate.

There is also inadvertent trapping, for example of dolphins and leatherback turtles in driftnets. The RSPCA has suggested that the problem could be greatly reduced if all driftnets were prohibited outside the 12km coastal limit. Migratory birds are deliberately trapped in some European countries and this is also a cruel and indiscriminate practice.

Box 6.2 *Concerns about pest control*

Some major pest control programmes have created unexpected welfare concerns, which have been widely expressed but for which no particular welfare organization has a specific responsibility. Two of them stem from the premature release in Australia of possible pest control agents.

1 Myxomatosis
In the 1950s, myxomatosis – a mosquito-borne disease – was prematurely released and caused the deaths of millions of rabbits. The reason for seeking an effective control was to eliminate the vast damage rabbits caused to native vegetation (at a cost of A$120m = US$89m a year, in 1995). However, the suffering and unpleasant deaths suffered by the rabbits caused considerable public revulsion and, ultimately, control proved ineffective as the rabbit population built up an immunity to the disease and recovered almost to its pre-myxomatosis level.

2 Rabbit Calcivirus Disease
Rabbit calcivirus disease (RCD) was prematurely released in Australia two years before it was due to be officially released as a means of biological control. It was subsequently released in New Zealand in 1997. The escape of the virus may have been due to the spread of bush flies from Wardang Island, where it was being tested, aided by strong southerly winds.

Millions of rabbits have died but one of the consequences has been that all their predators such as foxes and feral cats found their feed supply greatly reduced and started to prey on other creatures. This 'prey-switching' may threaten the survival of some native mammals, so it has become a conservation issue.

This example illustrates the unforeseen consequences of a virus which, apparently, only affected the target species.

Box 6.3 *Pest Control Research*

Amongst the great volume of animal welfare research carried out in research institutes and university departments all over the world, there is a significant amount concerned with devising more welfare-friendly methods of vertebrate pest control.

   An interesting example concerns the control of the Australian brushtail possum (Eason et al, 1998), which is considered to be the most damaging animal pest in New Zealand. Although the public supports control, there is strong feeling that it should be humane. Research is aimed at exploring alternative methods, as shooting and trapping are restricted to accessible areas, biological control may not be available for many years and poisoning may affect other animals as well. Currently, the best approach seems to be a combination of trapping and humane toxic baits.

If animals are to be returned to the wild, there are additional problems of rehabilitation and relocation into suitable areas. Wildlife casualties in the UK are monitored by the British Wildlife Rehabilitation Council, which has found that 25 per cent of cases submitted to centres are abandoned young and 63 per cent were thought to have been injured by human activity. Between 50 and 75 per cent of cases survived the first 48 hours and 35 to 60 per cent were subsequently released.

   Kirkwood and Best (1998) considered that rehabilitation of wildlife casualties is unlikely to be relevant to species conservation and may interfere with natural selection, but recognized that the case for intervention is more compelling where the illness or injury has been caused by human action.

   In some cases, however desirable, release to the wild may not be feasible. Animals may be permanently injured, incapable of feeding themselves, or simply have been in captivity too long. It may not be possible to return them to their original environments, which may no longer exist, and relevant environments may have no 'vacancies', being already fully populated with that particular species. Whether the environment has spare capacity may be hard to establish, especially for large predators with very large ranges and for deep sea animals including dolphins and killer whales. It is not a simple matter for a captive animal to readjust to life in the wild and this is particularly the case where it has been born in captivity. They have to be immune to the diseases they will encounter: it is also important that they do not spread new diseases into the wild population. Detailed protocols for release need to be followed.

Organizations Concerned with the Release of Captive Animals

Many organizations worldwide are involved in the release of captive animals, sometimes associated with captive breeding for the conservation of species in zoos. The reintroduction of species, following successful captive breeding, often involves animals that have spent their whole lives in zoos or in protected areas. The main issues are:

- Where are they to be released and how gradually?
- Will the habitat be suitable for the species and still have capacity to absorb new individuals? (In other words, if it is suitable, why isn't it full up?)
- Can the released animals feed themselves; avoid or cope with pests, parasites, predators and disease; and avoid continued dependence on humans or attack by them?
- Will released animals spread new diseases to the existing wild population?
- Will released animals upset the existing ecological balance?

It should be noted that most of these problems are greater if animals have been in captivity a long time – a problem that results from the closure of zoos, menageries and dolphinaria for example – and this is a major concern of WSPA.

There are also worries about disturbing the existing gene pool in the wild population and many people consider that released animals should only be returned to the areas and populations from which they came. This may not always be possible and, in any case, there may be no 'room'. It is also felt that released animals should be monitored, but this presents problems of such complexity that some hold the view that either release will rarely make sense or that continued captivity (let us assume, in improved conditions) will generally be preferable.

Before any species is considered for release, unless due to an accident, for example, it has only been out of its natural environment for a short period, a written protocol should be produced that answers satisfactorily all the above questions. It is also wise to circulate widely a draft of this protocol, first because other experts may be able to contribute and improve the draft and, secondly, because release operations are then less likely to be subjected to damaging public criticism. The confidence of the public can easily be lost if these precautions are not taken.

There may also be other questions that should be asked. The timing of release may be critical in terms of season, or even time of day or night, and the reproductive cycles of both released and other animals of the same species may need to be considered. Very often, release has to be done gradually, to accustom animals to the new situation and allow time for them to learn how to feed themselves, to meet the neighbours and demonstrate that they can survive: permanent dependence on supplementary feeding has to be avoided. All this can be expensive, especially if it involves transport of large animals such as elephants, giraffes, camels, dolphins or whales. Sometimes it may not be possible at all, and in such cases sanctuaries are needed (see Box 6.4).

Organizations Concerned with the Prevention of Cruelty

In some cases, cruel practices are allowed in a particular country (see Table 6.4) and change may require campaigns to influence politicians, practitioners or the public.

Sometimes these practices are associated with traditional cultural or religious festivals or long-established 'sports' and entertainments. Examples of these are given in Table 6.4 but it does not follow that other countries are not also involved or that those listed are the worst.

The WSPA is prominent in campaigns to ban such practices in many countries, having an international membership of more than 300, including the RSPCA (UK and Australia); Massachusetts SPCA; American Humane Association (AHA); American Society for the Prevention of Cruelty to Animals (ASPCA); Humane Society of the United States (HSUS); Deutscher Tierschutzbund (Germany); Schweizer Tierschutz (STS); Wiener Tierschutzverein (Austria); Ned Ver tot Bescherming van Dieren (NVBD) of The Netherlands.

Box 6.4 *The Need for Sanctuaries*

It may not be possible to release to the wild animals that have long been in captivity. Quite apart from the effects of isolation, they may have become old, weak, unfit or psychologically damaged. All this can happen to animals kept in captivity, whether caged or not.

Bears, for example, are used for bile production for use in traditional medicine in China, are exhibited as 'dancing' bears in Eastern Europe (especially in Greece, Turkey, Bulgaria, Russia, Romania) and in India. When such animals are rescued, amongst all their other problems, they may lack teeth and claws which have been removed to reduce their capacity to damage captors and have had rings and chains fixed to sensitive parts of the body. Many failed zoos leave a legacy of starving, sick, diseased and injured animals that require treatment, care, protection and a long period of recovery if it is possible to save them.

Exotic pets such as chelonians, snakes, small mammals, however badly they have been treated, cannot simply be returned to the wild since they may no longer be able to feed themselves or avoid predators.

Many animals such as donkeys, horses, ponies and guide dogs that may have been well treated during their working lives represent a problem when the owner no longer wants them.

In all the above cases, some form of sanctuary such as the Donkey Sanctuary in the UK is required so that the animals can end their lives with dignity and in an atmosphere of care. This does not mean, of course, that animals should be kept alive whatever the degree of suffering old age may bring.

Elephants, bears, large cats and wolves are animals living in social groups requiring wide ranges and specific environments in which poor human populations may be struggling to farm.

Organizations Concerned with Disease Control

Disease control is a major requirement for good welfare, preferably by prevention but also by cure, when that is necessary. The veterinary profession is the major force directed to the prevention and control of disease in all kinds of animals. It is a highly regulated profession and operates at all levels: in government programmes, private practice, commercial organizations and animal welfare bodies. Members

Table 6.4 *Cultural Festivals involving Cruelty*

Country	Practice
Belgium	Horse racing, donkey races, duck decapitation, cow fights, cock-fighting (although illegal since 1929)
Czech Republic	Horse race with extremely dangerous jumps and obstacles
El Salvador	Cow rodeo ('Jaripeo') in which the tongue of a young cow is bitten and pulled out by a clown
India	Dancing bears. About 3000 gypsies, known as 'Kalanders', claim that this is their only source of income
Japan	Horse lifting festival in which drugged horses are forced to jump at a vertical wall, resulting in many injuries
Mexico	Goat slaughter festival on October 22 in the State of Puebla
Pakistan and Greece	Bear-baiting (although illegal in Pakistan) continues: bears, tethered by a nose-ring and with their teeth removed, are repeatedly attacked by pairs of dogs
Spain	Fiesta in Castalon involves stabbing a bull to death after fitting exploding fireworks to its horns; goats thrown from church towers; chickens beheaded by blindfolded children; rabbits stoned to death
Spain, Mexico City, Colombia and other Latin American countries	Bullfighting: 492 fights in 1985, 720 fights in 1994 in Spain alone
US (Arizona, Illinois and Nevada)	Horse-tripping rodeos (Charreadas)

of the veterinary profession are increasingly concerned with positive welfare going well beyond the control of injury and disease.

The veterinary profession is therefore at the heart of all major animal care activities and is involved in all aspects of disease prevention and control and also has concerns about animal welfare outside disease control. There are, however, two major problems. The first is that veterinary treatment, however necessary, cannot always be afforded.

Very poor people, for example, often simply do not have the money to take their pet to a vet for treatment. Pets are very important to the health and well-being of many people, especially the old and lonely, and they may be very important to children. Fortunately, there are charities, such as the PDSA and Blue Cross, that will pay for the treatment of animals belonging to those genuinely unable to afford it themselves. But such services are not generally available to commercial operators, such as farmers, and, when profitability is low, veterinary treatment may prove too expensive. In 1998, UK vets in general practice spent 66 per cent of their total working time on small animals and the proportion of time spent on farm animals has diminished since that time.

A quite different case is represented by numerous, low-value farm animals, especially poultry but also maybe sheep, where the value of the animal, in a commercial context, does not justify treatment. Such animals would normally be killed rather than receive treatment or be subjected to continue suffering.

As in human medicine, veterinary treatment has become increasingly sophisticated and expensive, so that many things are now possible which were not so only a short time ago. Examples include hip replacement in ageing dogs; cancer treatments using chemotherapy and radiotherapy; neurosurgery (only feasible following computed tomography (CT) or magnetic resonance imaging (MRI) scanning); and organ transplantation (performed in the US but not yet in the UK). People who can afford it may now pay for hip replacement in dogs or neurosurgery and who can say that they should not? Vets enjoy the challenge (and the income) represented by exercising skills at the limit of their professional competence, so scarce resources may be diverted in these directions. What is wrong with that?

But the use of resources in these ways raises problems, as it does with humans, and treatment may involve painful procedures, about which the animal cannot be consulted. Costs can be considerable. For example a CT scanner costs some £10,000 secondhand but the cost of transportation and installation is likely to be more than double that. Two large rooms and three-phase power supply are involved and significant power costs incurred. Maintenance contracts start at about £36,000 per year, quite apart from the occasional need for, say, a new X-ray tube at a further £36,000.

Trained staff are needed and there are additional processing costs. At an average of ten cases per week, it has been estimated (Boydell and Crossley, 1997) that a charge of £300 would be necessary per case, to which must be added VAT and the costs of tests, examinations, anaesthesia etc.

Across all these categories, governments and local authorities are involved and the legislative framework is voluminous and complex. An example of the valuable work of local authorities in the UK is the introduction of dog wardens, which has reduced the number of pets kept in unsuitable conditions and the number of 'latchkey' dogs (dogs turned out in numbers in large inner city council estates, which is now no longer a problem).

Education

All operators and keepers of animals need to be equipped to discharge their responsibilities. In the case of professionals, training is probably required: in the case of pet-keepers, it is education (see Box 6.5). There are some areas of special concern, especially for particular groups of animals.

Box 6.5 *Education in Animal Welfare*

There is now a wide range of educational establishments that provide courses in various aspects of animal welfare. Schools also have an important role in teaching children about welfare, particularly in relation to pets. However, there are also welfare problems arising out of the use of animals to 'visit' schools, animals kept captive at schools and visits to animal-related venues. The RSPCA believes that animals are best studied in their natural environments.

But there is also a huge need for the pet-keeping public to receive information about how best to keep their pets. The vast majority of people wish to treat their pets properly but they do not always know how to do it. Fortunately, TV programmes are helping, and many welfare organizations distribute advisory leaflets.

The pet industry as a whole, including pet superstores, manufacturers and retailers of pet food, pet insurers, veterinary practices and the pharmaceutical industry, is also promoting responsible pet ownership.

In the UK, the Pet Health Council, formed in 1979, was set up specifically to promote the health and welfare of pets, produces leaflets and offers a helpline to answer queries. Pets are, of course, a major concern in the UK. Over 11 million households (just under half of the total) own a pet of one kind or another. So educational programmes have a big role.

But there is a great need in other parts of the world, and the recent development of 'Kindness Clubs' by WSPA in Africa shows what can be done. These clubs combine education with clinics to treat animals and local participation in sanctuaries.

For farm livestock, welfare can suffer in markets, but other kinds of markets such as street stalls sell pets of all kinds and may be ill-equipped to care for the animals at the point of sale.

Transport is another area of concern, especially since it frequently involves more than one control zone (county, state, country). It may be by road, air or sea and each mode of transport has its own special problems, such as of duration of journey, stress, space, facilities for feeding and watering, loading and unloading, motion and exposure. People involved in many of these operations are not trained to deal with animals and, in some cases, may not be totally aware that animals are involved. Small animals, including monkeys, birds, tortoises, may be packed into small and quite inadequate containers where the contents are not declared.

Summary

1 There are, worldwide, 6–8000 bodies concerned with animal protection and welfare.
2 Some set standards, some are advisory, some exert control, some prosecute offenders, some monitor what is going on, some rescue injured animals, some are pressure groups on behalf of particular species, some provide sanctuaries for old or ill-treated animals, some provide veterinary treatment and some provide relevant education.
3 Such organizations provide a more powerful voice than individuals can generally muster and greatly increase the effectiveness of individual members or supporters.

7

Achieving Improvement

'There's always an easy solution to every human problem – neat, plausible, and wrong' (H L Mencken)

The whole purpose of studying animal welfare, thinking and writing about it, campaigning and organizing, is to improve the situation. So the best measures of success are the scale and rate of improvement, and this requires assessment of the problems and the extent of their solution. The sheer size and scale of the problems can easily have a profoundly depressing effect on all of us and leave us with a helpless feeling that nothing much can be done. The same is true of human suffering, injustice and cruelty, of course, and it is a responsibility of the citizen to face up to the problems and contribute to their solutions.

The first step in solving problems has to be their detailed identification. It is too easy to believe, sometimes strongly and emotionally, that both the problem and its solution are obvious.

In Chapter 6, the complexity of the situation was illustrated by the example of the release of captive animals. It may seem quite clear that an animal should not be captive, but for a particular animal it may be best that it remains in captivity. This does not mean that it should remain in the same conditions, of course, but it may not be right to release it. It is hard to quantify such matters accurately, but there is evidence of cases where releases have not been successful: so the percentage of successes needs to be high in order to justify release.

A different example is that of oil-polluted sea-birds. When major oil pollution disasters occur, the pitiful condition of the affected sea-birds cries out for action and it can be argued that we have nothing to lose, since untreated birds will certainly die. However, if treatment involves great stress and further suffering, euthanasia might be better. For some sea-bird species, the success rate is claimed to be poor, but it can be argued that it is all worthwhile if only a few are saved. We would say the same for rescuing human beings in the aftermath of major disaster. Wernham et al (1997) estimated that only one per cent mainly of de-oiled guillemots survived for one year after release; comparable figures from Camphuysen et al (1997) were 22 per cent. Other estimates, for other species, vary from 9 to 60 per cent.

Good survival has been found with the Jackass Penguin, the Cape Gannet, the Mute Swan and the Australian Little Penguin.

There is, however, an economic argument that we never have enough resources to do all we want, so there is good reason to spend money cost-effectively, because it might achieve more in other directions. The extent to which economics is relevant to animal welfare will be discussed later in this chapter.

At this point, we have only to recognize that not all welfare problems can be tackled at once and not all are of equal importance. Many organizations and conferences have identified what they believe to be priorities and, although none are able to say how the total array of problems should be prioritized, it is worth considering the ones that have been identified.

Priorities for Animal Welfare Improvement

It is not, in fact, necessary to arrive at an overall priority list, since different groups of people have different responsibilities and, in any case, there is not just one pot of money to be distributed. In the case of charities, people often contribute for a particular purpose, to support a specific campaign or to alleviate suffering in a particular species: the money donated has to be used for such purposes and might not be given for any other.

In the case of cats in the UK, for example, Cats Protection has quite specific objectives but it nonetheless has a sense of priorities within them. Recently, they have called for a major effort to neuter pet cats in an attempt to reduce the current number of strays. Tens of thousands of kittens are said to be 'thrown onto the streets' each year. They suffer from starvation and disease but manage to breed at an alarming rate. Of the 7.5 million cats in the UK, about one million are thought not be neutered.

The National Canine Defence League (NCDL) takes a similar view about dogs. Of 106,000 stray dogs rounded up between 1 April 1996 and 31 March 1997, one in six had to be destroyed. Of the rest, half were returned to their owners and 10 per cent found new homes. Proper identification (identity discs are required by law) would make return to owners much simpler.

So here we have an example, where two of our major welfare charities, dealing with our two most popular and numerous pets, are calling for neutering – in the interests of welfare. Yet, for farm animals, concern is quite the reverse, with FAWC finding all mutilations to be objectionable and calling for the development of livestock production systems that do not require castration. And in agriculture it is only the males that are neutered – a rather simpler operation.

The Eurogroup for Animal Welfare (1988) gave an analysis of the major areas of concern for animal welfare in Europe. For intensive livestock systems they identified inadequate provision of space for hens, sows and rabbits, and mutilations and lameness especially in cattle. In extensive systems the focus was on losses due to disease and exposure, and lack of attention at critical times.

The Council of Europe Convention for the Protection of Pet Animals prohibits surgical intervention solely to modify appearance. Transport and slaughter also gave cause for concern. There are now detailed controls in place in Europe, specifying journey times, lairage arrangements, stocking densities, and design of vehicles, but there are major concerns about implementation and policing. Inadequate loading and lairage facilities, poorly trained staff, poorly designed stunning pens and exemption from stunning for certain religious groups are the major welfare concerns arising from slaughter. Eurogroup for Animal Welfare (1988) also identified the following major welfare concerns for other animals:

- *Wildlife*
  Use of gin or steel-jawed leg-hold traps (prohibited in the UK, Eire, FDR, Italy and Portugal). Use of snares.
- *Fur-farming*
  Unsuitable cages.

- *Migratory and indigenous birds*
  Millions are killed annually. They are shot, snared, trapped, netted or caught with birdlime.
- *Marine mammals*
  Commercial killing of whales, dolphins and other cetaceans. The EU has not imported whale products since 1981 and protection is afforded under CITES.
- *Marine Turtles*
  Cruel methods of slaughter without stunning.
- *Kangaroos*
  Ten species are hunted in Australia and, on the scale involved, some methods are inhumane.
- *Equines*
  Transport; competitions with unreasonable jumps and obstacles and training and performance-enhancing medication.
- *Dogs*
  Mutilations such as ear cropping and tail docking.
- *Animals used in experiments*
  This is poorly regulated in many countries but a great deal of routine toxicity testing is required by health and safety legislation.
- *Animals used in sport and entertainment*
  Attention is drawn to bull-fighting (on behalf of both bulls and horses), fox hunting and hare coursing, use of animals in TV, films and video and wild animals used in beach photography.
- *Animals used for exotic foods*
  Welfare problems include the removal of legs from live frogs, and forced feeding of geese and ducks for pâté de foie gras. Genetic engineering is also mentioned (see also Chapter 10).

Clearly, some improvements have been achieved since 1988 but many more remain to be brought about. Part of the reason for this is the sheer difficulty of getting agreement across a large number of nations. Currently, advance in the EU requires agreement between fifteen nations, some four of which may be having a national election in any one year. Thus if we want Europe to move together, we have to accept slow progress.

Objections to small battery cages for laying hens have been voiced in many countries, including the UK, for about 30 years and we still await real change, although a decision to change has just (1999) been taken in Europe. There are reasons for this, including the lack of genuinely better alternatives for large-scale egg production, but welfarists would regard this as the best example of unreasonable delay and the sheer length of time that welfare progress takes. It is easy to see the frustration that this causes and how it generates the feeling that stronger action is needed in order to achieve progress.

However, individual countries are free to make such improvements as they choose, independent of the EU, as the UK did with the effective banning of narrow veal crates (1990) and of sow stalls and tethers (1999), and the Commission has now brought forward new proposals on both of these (see Box 7.1). What they cannot do, however, is prevent the importation of the same product from other countries on welfare grounds. Thus if an improvement increases the cost of production of farm livestock or the costs of research with laboratory animals or transport, or increases the price of the product (eg pets), home production may be damaged, or even wiped out, whilst the same product is imported because it is cheaper.

Box 7.1 *EU Commission Proposals on Veal Crates and Sow Stalls*

1 Veal crates
From 1 January 1998 all newly-built or rebuilt holdings are obliged to follow new rules, including the following:

1   No calf shall be confined in an individual pen after the age of eight weeks: the width of the pen shall be at least equal to the height of the calf at the withers and the length equal to its length. Pens must not have solid walls.
2   Calves kept in groups should have space of at least 1.5 to 1.8m^2 for each calf, depending on its liveweight.

The white-veal crate will be effectively banned in the EU from 1 January 2006.

2 Sow stalls
Sow tethers will be banned in the EU from 2006 but stalls can continue. The UK has banned both from 1999. A recent EU report concluded that sow welfare was better when they were kept in groups rather than being confined in stalls. The advantages of groups included more exercise and opportunity for social interaction, less abnormal bone and muscle development, less abnormal behaviour and better cardio-vascular fitness.

Consumers may often declare that they want welfare improved but then actually purchase what is cheapest, wherever it comes from. Very often products come from countries where the production process is worse for animal welfare than the home production system was before it was banned. As a result, the action taken results not in solving the welfare problem but exporting it to another country, which then increases the objectionable practice to meet the new demand. The brake on unilateral action is therefore not merely economic but has an important welfare dimension.

FAWC, for example, makes the same recommendation as does government that 'battery cages should not be banned' until certain conditions are met (see Box 7.2). Sweden, having decided to ban battery cages by 1 January 1999, now finds that alternative systems are not satisfactory without beak-trimming (which is not permitted in Sweden). Its solution is to ban the original battery cage but to allow a modified form (about 90 per cent of Swedish eggs are produced in battery cages).

A comparable process has been going on to change the status of animals in the 1957 Treaty of Rome, the cornerstone of EU law. The treaty classified animals as goods or 'agricultural products'.

In 1991, a petition signed by over one million people from all the Community's Member States was presented by Compassion in World Farming to the President of the European Parliament, to change the status of animals to that of 'sentient beings'. In January 1994 the European Parliament endorsed the petition's request and in 1997 the decision was made to incorporate the necessary changes.

This difficulty of harmonization of controls within the EU is paralleled by international trade agreements relating to free trade.

It took seven years to complete the most recent 'Uruguay' round of negotiations and the General Agreement on Tariffs and Trade (GATT). It is based on the principle that trade should be non-discriminatory and that national legislation should not aim to give domestic producers an economic advantage over its competitors. There are some areas, such as environment and animal health – but not animal welfare – where exceptions are allowed. In 1995, the GATT was replaced by the WTO.

A further round of negotiations began in 1999 in Seattle, but little progress was made, and none at all in incorporating considerations of animal welfare.

Box 7.2 *Summary of FAWC Recommendations Concerning Battery Cages for Laying Hens*

Battery cages which do not provide a nest box, perch or litter arguably cause hens frustration and suffering. It may be that battery cages in their present form should be phased out throughout the EU if hens can be practically provided with greater space, nests, perches and possibly scratching, foraging and dust bathing facilities in other systems without increasing injurious pecking.

FAWC is of the opinion that the use of conventional battery cages should be phased out in the long term with the following provisos, which should be energetically pursued:

- The UK industry must be protected from unfair competition from elsewhere within the EU; phasing out throughout the EU must take place simultaneously.
- Imports of shell eggs and egg products into the EU must be banned from those countries in which conventional battery cages are still used. The General Agreement on Tariffs and Trade and World Trade Organization (GATT/WTO) arrangements should not be allowed to prevent these measures and, if necessary, the UK Government should seek an amendment to the agreement in order to protect the welfare of animals.
- There are signs that genetic selection for reduced injurious pecking behaviour may remove an obstacle to the widespread use of non-cage systems. The phasing out of battery cages should not be effected until after the elimination or successful control of injurious pecking and cannibalism through genetic progress or improvements to management technique.

Source: FAWC, 1997

Progress is thus possible and campaigns often succeed, but we have to recognise that they take time, not only to obtain agreement to change but further time to achieve implementation. This is particularly clear in agriculture, where physical facilities may involve substantial financial investment and cannot be changed radically overnight. Much legislation therefore includes transition periods, often of up to ten years, to allow changes to be made. Normally this only applies to existing systems, new ones having to conform immediately.

This kind of delay can be abused and it is often suspected that change could be more rapid if the will was there. Indeed, it normally occurs very rapidly if there is any economic incentive to be gained. This problem is acute where change has to depend upon the development of better alternatives, since these may be deliberately delayed. A proper assessment of the cost of welfare improvement is thus of vital importance.

The Economics of Welfare Improvement

The economics of welfare improvement have been mostly applied to farm livestock production systems (see McInerney, 1994), but the principles are the same for all forms of commercial exploitation of animals. If welfare is reduced by cost-saving measures that increase profit there is clearly a temptation to adopt them.

Turning a dog out on to the streets when it has outgrown its attractive puppyhood in order to save the unexpectedly higher cost of feeding it is little different from keeping fur animals in the smallest possible cages in order to reduce housing costs. There are some differences, however. In the case of pets, it may be that they have become dangerous or valueless for other reasons. In farming, the calculation is made as to whether profit will be increased or decreased, and it is argued that no profit means bankruptcy and less profit may mean failure to compete with others.

In the case of livestock production, it is widely assumed that better welfare always costs money, but this is not so. There are many cases where better welfare means higher production and greater profit, even if it does cost money. This is so for better transport of pigs to slaughter, avoiding the stress that actually reduces the quality and value of the meat produced. There are also recently documented cases where simply friendlier treatment of pigs resulted in faster growth rates and better reproductive success of sows (European Commission, 1997). Not only does such treatment cost nothing, it may actually increase the job satisfaction of the stockman.

Worldwide, widespread ill-treatment of animals results from ignorance, callousness, habit or thoughtlessness and may well be counter-productive and even costly: it costs nothing to change such human attitudes although, in practice, it may require education and training. More than forty years ago, it was established that changing the cowman had a marked effect on milk yield of the same cows under the same conditions.

Training of animals (see Chapter 5) is also more effective if based on kindness and rewards rather than punishment. A discussion paper produced by Professor English for FAWC has shown training of stockpersons improves pig output on farms in the UK by 11.7 to 12.6 per cent, with significantly greater growth rates.

Of course, as noted earlier, competition from worse but cheaper production systems does place a constraint on progress, but it is wrong to assume automatically that better welfare will be too costly. Even where this is a cost, it may lead to improved and profitable performance, but the cost is not necessarily to be borne by the producer: it could be borne by consumers who genuinely wish to see animal welfare improved.

Small battery cages for laying hens are a good example. A farmer's common response takes the form of, 'Certainly you can have more welfare-friendly eggs, if you're prepared to pay twice as much for them.' Quite apart from the uncaring image this creates and the reinforcement in the public's mind that what they pay is what the farmer gets (the farmer generally receives less than half the retail price), it grossly exaggerates the cost/price consequence.

Production costs are only part of the total cost of providing food for sale. Transport, processing and actually selling the products also contribute to the total. So an increase in production costs should not, by itself, result in a proportionate increase in the retail price. According to Stevenson (1997), free-range hens' eggs cost only 1.4 pence per egg more than battery eggs and, since we each eat about 1.85 eggs per week, the extra cost would be 2.6 pence per person per week, an increase of 0.19 per cent in our overall expenditure on food. This is an up-to-date calculation, but Elson (1985) calculated an index of production costs (with battery cages = 100) of 108 to 118 for perchery, aviary and deep litter systems, 130 to 140 for straw yard and semi-intensive systems, and 170 for free-range systems. It therefore seems that the costs of free-range systems have come down. Now, of course, all these figures are dependent upon stocking densities and other factors, but it is clear that some improved systems need not cost that much more and the retail price need not be excessive.

In other cases, there may be a large initial capital cost, such as building longer cubicles to cater for the longer modern cows. Some improved welfare systems may actually offer financial advantages. Outdoor breeding of pigs is an example, but it cannot be carried out on all soil types and under all weather conditions. In other words, there is evidence that it pays to be humane (Carruthers, 1991); but this is not always so. What is needed is open-minded research aimed at devising better welfare systems that are also profitable.

The need for improved welfare is also relevant to public activities such as farming and zoos, and to private activities such as pet-keeping in homes and in animals laboratories. The emphasis on welfare is because cruelty (in the UK at least) is against the law, though not for the majority of wild animals. Broom (1992) pointed out that it was not against UK law to pull the legs off a hedgehog in the wild, because the Protection of Animals Act did not include wild animals. This would strike most people as both reprehensible and extraordinary, but the law as an agent for change represents a rather limited way of ensuring a safety net, setting the very minimum standards of behaviour. Fortunately, in 1996, the Wild Mammals (Protection) Act corrected the situation, at least for mammals.

Cruelty to pets is against the law but that does not prevent it happening. The RSPCA National Cruelty Statistics for 1996 revealed that the number of people jailed in the UK for cruelty to animals increased by over 100 per cent from 1995 to 1996. Total convictions were 2282, and cruelty was widespread: dogs 892 cases, cats 235, horses and donkeys 128, cattle 186, sheep 168, pigs 65 and wildlife 121.

Clearly then, charities such as the RSPCA represent a major force for change, and individuals can help to achieve welfare improvements by supporting them.

What and who are the main agents for change?

Agents for Welfare Improvement

All the organizations referred to in Chapter 6 play their part in advising government on the need for legislation, on formulating standards and codes, on conducting research to improve our understanding of both needs and how to meet them, by protecting, rescuing and rehabilitating animals and so on. In turn, charities' activities can be monitored by their supporters, and the public (and pressure groups) can monitor the actions of government agencies and local authorities. Quality assurance groups and trade associations will increasingly be involved in ensuring that proper standards are followed by their members. But we are not totally dependent on the widely-known bodies and there are other agents for welfare improvement, as described in the following sections.

Individual Action

If livestock products are not purchased, they will not be produced: the consumer is all powerful. This power of the purchaser applies just as much to paying for puppies, tortoises and visits to zoos as it does to bacon or eggs. (It is true that more knowledge is actually required to exert consumer pressure on the use of equipment such as cages, feed or fencing.)

If we wished, we could refuse to buy meat, milk, eggs, wool and fur and a host of derived products unless they were guaranteed to come from good welfare systems. Why don't we do that?

In some cases it is simply ignorance; others will say that they cannot afford to be so choosy; some that they don't care, or that they don't think it will make any difference, and, of course, that is true if only one or two people act. But we surely ought to do what we believe to be right, irrespective of how many others are doing it.

Pressure Groups

In the case of speaking out, lobbying or demonstrating, there is no doubt that it is more effective for individuals to combine, and pressure groups exist to focus opinion in a targeted way, mobilizing public opinion to press for specific changes. In general, pressure groups can gain sufficient publicity because of their views and supporting facts: they do not need to depend upon sensational or outrageous behaviour.

A major advantage that pressure groups have over individuals is that they can carry out fact-finding exercises, but it is not always easy to gain access to all the information needed. For example, laboratories and their suppliers are not normally open to public inspection and, often for reasons of disease control or disturbance to the animals, the same is true of many intensive livestock enterprises, especially poultry and pig houses.

There are also cases where undercover camera work has been required to establish facts which would not otherwise have been allowed to be filmed. This emphasizes the point that for practitioners to be trusted, there has to be openness to the limit that is possible and, even where access is not feasible, means have to be found to ensure that nothing remains hidden, confidentiality notwithstanding. Pressure groups therefore depend upon public support and this will only be forthcoming if they respect the law and normal standards of fair play.

Government

Government, as already mentioned, can only provide through legislation a safety net to ensure compliance with minimum standards, but it does have a role in education and encouragement of better behaviour by individuals and organizations. After all, the government should be the voice of its citizens and articulate the standards of behaviour that society wishes to abide by. However, as has also already been pointed out, governments are limited by international agreements as to what they can legislate for and how fast they can move. In addition, in some countries (eg US and Australia) legislation may vary from state to state. Governments are, for these reasons, unlikely to be in the forefront of animal welfare improvement or, at least, we should not rely on them being at the cutting edge, driving things forward. Others are increasingly taking up that role.

The Retailers

In the UK, the major retailers have enormous power and they have decided to use it to raise the welfare standards involved in the production of what they sell. They have all declared their intention to source their animal products only from suppliers who conform to agreed animal welfare standards. For livestock products, these standards are mainly based on FAWC recommendations, although it may not be immediately possible to implement them all in full. But the potential of this development for rapid progress in welfare improvement is such that we should welcome it while recognizing that everything cannot be achieved overnight.

The retailers have several crucial advantages over government in this context:

- They can move faster.
- Their power is not limited by national boundaries: it applies wherever in the world they source their supplies.
- They are not bound by international trade agreements in the same way that governments are.
- They have great power: if a supplier does not conform, his contract can be cancelled and this can represent his livelihood.
- They have mechanisms for checking on standards: they already inspect their sources for food safety, quality and hygiene.

It may be suspected that these claims may not be genuine and may not apply to all products. The latter will certainly be so, initially. The former seems unlikely. Having publicly committed themselves to such a programme, they cannot afford to be caught out – and there will be no shortage of hawk-eyed observers, including their competitors, looking for failures of compliance. Their reputations are on the line and these are their most valuable assets. This being so, suppliers also cannot afford to be caught out, since this will risk their livelihood. It is important to recognize that everything in this endeavour depends upon trust.

There is no possibility of putting all the details of the relevant welfare standards on the label attached to the product: the details are too numerous, space would not allow it and customers would find it difficult to digest such a mass of small print or to understand and interpret it. What both retailer and customer want is trust in the assurance that the product has come from welfare-friendly systems.

Trust always has to be earned over time but there are two initial conditions that have to be satisfied:

1 That the standards are not set in-house but are based on those set by established, authoritative and independent bodies. FAWC is one such body for farm animals and the RSPCA Freedom Foods Scheme is a major step in bridging the gap between FAWC recommendations and standards that can be operated by a retailer immediately.
2 It is essential that some degree of independent monitoring occurs. A wholly in-house arrangement would simply not be credible.

The Media

All kinds of media have a role in educating citizens, in alerting them to areas of concern, in publicizing the activities of all the main players and encouraging support for those trying to improve matters.

The dangers are those of oversimplifying very complex issues, of stirring up emotions to the point that they obscure the facts and of encouraging confrontation rather than cooperation. Confrontation is counter-productive and results in increased polarization and, fatally, failure to listen to other points of view. Not listening to moderates generates extremists, who may even have the passive support of the moderates because 'we got nowhere!' Unfortunately, a moderate can almost be defined as someone who can be safely ignored – which is what happens too often. People who are not listened to, or not taken seriously, will not trust those who ignore them.

The greatest need for those wishing to improve the welfare of all animals is to become involved, one way or another, recognizing that the majority of people want the same thing, though they may disagree about the precise nature of problems and solutions.

We have to find ways in which such differences can be debated in an informed and calm manner; we have to listen to each other and devise ways in which cooperation can displace confrontation.

Research

We depend upon research to advance our understanding of the physiology and nutrition of animals and how they perceive welfare and to devise better systems for keeping animals, particularly those kept in captivity and on farms.

Physiology and Nutrition

The Roslin Institute in Edinburgh is studying the welfare of birds, including genetic selection for reduced feather-pecking. It should not be forgotten that aggression is a major obstacle to the development of many potentially welfare-friendly poultry systems, in which, currently, feather-pecking has to be controlled by beak-trimming.

Fear responses – to unexpected noise or movement – can cause injury and pain, and fearful birds are more difficult to manage, are slow to adapt to environmental change, and show poorer growth, egg production and product quality. In Japanese quail, for example, it is possible to select for less fearful birds and there is some evidence that fearfulness and growth rate are negatively related (but this may turn out to be more complicated). If it was true that less fearful birds also grow faster, this would be another example of the interests of the bird and the keeper coinciding.

So commercial requirements may not always conflict with good welfare, although there is always the concern that animals could be bred not to object to the ways we treat them. This coincidence of interest is also reflected in the disposal of unwanted male chicks. Since male and female chicks are produced in equal numbers but only the latter are wanted for laying systems, the surplus males have to be disposed of (see also Chapter 4). Poultry meat producers, however, would prefer all male birds because of their faster growth and greater food conversion efficiency.

Sexing and disposal are both welfare concerns and they involve economic costs. If the sex could be determined, as it can in some reptiles, by temperature adjustment, both welfare and economics would benefit.

Better Systems and Practices

The effects of some practices, undesirable in themselves but currently still necessary, can be limited by sensible use.

For example, teeth clipping in piglets is often done routinely but could be restricted only to those cases where the sow does not allow the piglets to drink, something which becomes apparent within 24 hours of birth. (Teeth clipping can cause canine teeth to splinter, thus exposing pulp cavities in the milk teeth, which are not replaced by permanent teeth until the animals are one year old.)

Slight modification to equipment can also achieve major improvements, as for example to the cages of breeding doe rabbits. Rabbits are normally shy and retiring and, in cages, they lack privacy and exercise, as well as any stimulation. Group housing systems have now been developed in Switzerland (Stauffacher, 1985 and 1992) to house five does, one buck and pre-weaned kits (a natural unit), with compartments and nest boxes, including a compartment to which only the kits have access. The systems appear to work well but are not yet commercially feasible.

Modified cages, aviaries and percheries are also being developed for hens and could eventually replace battery cages.

Summary

1   The whole purpose of concern about animal welfare is to improve it.
2   We must not be put off by the sheer size, scale and complexity of the problems or the idea that we cannot make a difference.
3   However, we have to recognize that the best way to improve welfare is by no means obvious.
4   We should only pursue actions that will be effective. There is no point in taking actions that make us feel better but do not benefit the target animals.
5   Sometimes it is necessary for individuals and for nations to band together in order to be effective.
6   It is necessary to try and understand all the costs and consequences of proposed actions.
7   In some cases, we may lack the knowledge necessary to decide what should be done: research may then be needed to put this right.

8

Action Needed

'If you think that education is expensive, try ignorance' (English proverb)

In order to discharge responsibilities in relation to animal welfare, a citizen clearly needs to become adequately informed about the main issues and how things can be improved. The latter embraces changes that need to be made to the ways in which animals are kept and treated, in order that their welfare can be improved, and also what action is needed in order to bring about those changes.

Different actions are needed to address different problems, relating to the nature of the problem, the kind of animal involved, where in the world it is kept and by whom, and the route by which change can best be achieved. Earlier chapters have tried to deal with such matters, to the extent that one book, in plain language, can cover such a wide range of issues. In some areas, such as education and training, the requirement is across the board, and needs continuing, steady pressure to ensure that, wherever animals are involved, those dealing with them should be adequately trained and those influencing policy and regulation should be adequately educated. All this depends upon an appreciation that animals are capable of suffering and that animal welfare matters. Unfortunately, neither of these can be assumed and, to many people, such propositions would be new and unfamiliar.

Where it is accepted that an understanding of animal welfare is an essential part of what it means to be a citizen, then it should form part of that citizen's education from the earliest age. Indeed, how to treat pets and other animals properly and humanely is part of growing up and begins pre-school. In other words, there is here a parental responsibility, especially (but not only) in households with pets, and parents have to be adequately informed in order to discharge it.

Learning about Animal Welfare at School

There are additional needs and problems at school. Busy teachers are bound to find it difficult, in addition to all their other responsibilities, to deal with the complexities of animal welfare. Yet they, and the children, are exposed to propaganda from all sides, with vested-interest groups of all kinds wanting to ensure that their point of view is represented. Some of these groups are able to supply attractive literature, with reassuring or horrifying pictures that can have a big impact on both teachers and taught.

It would be worth a lot of thought as to how all this could be done better, at all educational levels. Clearly, the ideal is a balanced account that recognizes what is wrong but also what is good and what can be done to make it better. In 'visiting animal schemes', there are concerns about overhandling of individual animals, inadequate caging and transport between schools. Within schools, better supervision may be needed at weekends and in school holidays.

Dissection

One special problem at school, and at higher levels of education for some students, is dissection. The whole problem of 'living biology in schools' has recently been reviewed (Reiss, 1996), including details about what procedures are permitted by law, which species are legally protected and attitudes to dissection. The arguments for dissection of dead animals include:

- It is the best way to understand how internal structures relate to one another.
- It involves learning through active involvement.
- It involves learning about what certain careers in medicine and veterinary science might entail.

Arguments against are:

• It may involve taking life.
• It may involve rearing animals simply in order to be killed to produce the necessary specimens.
• It lessens respect for life.
• It offends some pupils and their fellows.
• It may put some pupils off biology, most of which does not involve dissection.

It is recommended that children should always be free to choose and that dissection is inappropriate for those under the age of 11. Children should be free to discuss frankly their attitudes and the ethical implications. In the UK pupils should be told that dissection is not required by examining boards. Alternatives to dissection should be available.

The issues are somewhat different later, when students have chosen a particular area of study or a career, since a completely free choice may not be possible, desirable or even safe. After all, at some point a newly qualified doctor or veterinary surgeon may have to operate on a live patient.

Zinko, Jukes and Gericke (1997) list alternative methods for educational use. This book also describes 'Euroniche', an international network of teachers, students and others working to end the use of animals in undergraduate education: the network extends over more than 20 countries.

Companion Animals

In addition to the need for education in the keeping of companion animals and the need to establish an independent advisory body (see later in this chapter), there are special difficulties in the ways in which exotic pets are obtained.

'Unusual' animals such as parrots, reptiles, marine fish and mammals are often acquired directly from the wild. Many (eg 75 per cent of wild birds) die due to inhumane collection methods and poor travelling conditions. Millions of ornamental fish are involved.

The trade in endangered species is controlled, to some extent, by CITES (see Box 5.3) but this is not always effective and it has recently been reported (Burrell, 1998) that animal smuggling is now the most lucrative crime after drugs. It would be better if a permit was required to keep exotic species and its issue depended on demonstrated competence.

Animals in Research

The use of animals in research and testing, which may be routine, is controlled in the UK, but this is not so worldwide.

There are campaigns based on the Three Rs – Replacement, Reduction and Refinement (see Matfield, 1996a, for a short history), and there is wide agreement that alternatives should be sought. There is increasing hope that alternatives will become steadily more available. These include *in vitro* as opposed to *in vivo* methods, using single animal cells, cultures or bacteria, and the use of organs from dead animals, computer simulations, and the use of invertebrates, but there are new areas of research opening up (see Chapter 9) that involve new forms of animal experimentation.

In some areas, however, there appears to be a strong case for abolition of the use of animals in experiments. Where animals are used, there ought to be a requirement that people involved should be adequately trained, and this should include consideration of the Three Rs.

Cosmetics Testing

Many people see little or no justification for using animals for testing cosmetic products and ingredients. Those that believe them to be necessary argue that the law may require such testing to be carried out and that the safety of the human user demands it. However, some 500 ingredients have already been tested and few cosmetics can be regarded as essential for human welfare. The arguments for cosmetics testing are therefore much weaker than for medicines for humans and animals – see next section.

The EU recognized public concern and proposed to ban animal testing for cosmetic products and ingredients as from 1 January 1998, provided that scientifically-validated alternative non-animal tests were available. The matter, however, has been postponed because of commercial objections. The European Parliament, which wanted implementation by the agreed date, has received a petition signed by four million EU residents demanding an end to cosmetics testing. As the RSPCA and Eurogroup for Animal Welfare Memorandum (1997) pointed out, progress has been slow and the matter is still not resolved. The Eurogroup is urging the Council of Ministers to confirm implementation of the ban as laid down in the Amendment to Directive 76/768/EEC.

The use of animals for testing cosmetics and their ingredients was banned in the UK in 1998. However, it always has to be remembered that banning an activity in one country or group of countries may simply mean that it is carried out somewhere else.

The Use of Animals in Medicine

Medical research aims to learn more about how the body functions, about the prevention, control and cure of disease, about the repair of injuries and failures of parts of the body, about avoiding painful or damaging conditions and increasing the quality of life.

All these are laudable objectives and medical progress over the years has been, and continues to be, spectacular.

Examples of progress in medicine due to animal experimentation include development of vaccines, transplant of organs, scanning machines, life support systems for kidney, heart and lung machines, and the testing of drugs for reduction of blood pressure.

Medical advances in which the use of animals has been involved include the development of insulin for diabetics, modern anaesthetics for surgery, penicillin, polio vaccine (using monkeys), hip replacements, drugs for schizophrenia, ulcers and asthma, life support systems for premature babies, vaccine for leprosy (using armadillos), coronary by-pass and open-heart surgery (using dogs), and vaccine for measles, German measles and whooping cough.

It is argued that fundamental research on animals has led to major advances because our biological understanding has been increased: it is also argued that it would be wrong to sell or use modern treatments that have not been first tested on animals to determine safety, dose rates and frequency, and side-effects for example. Counter-arguments are that humans are different and what is appropriate for other animals may not be so for us.

There should be no disagreement, however, that alternatives should be used wherever possible, and where animals have to be used, suffering should be minimized. It must also be remembered that parallel arguments are made for research that has benefited animals.

Advances in veterinary medicine that it is claimed (Carter and Rickard, 1998) have depended on animal-based research include vaccines for anthrax, tetanus, botulism, blackleg, black disease and enterotoxaemia; control of contagious bovine pleuropneumonia (eradicated in Australia in the 1960s); and the control of TB and brucellosis, fleas, and internal parasites.

Vaccination now provides protection from diseases in cats, dogs, horses, cattle, sheep, pigs and poultry.

Conditions and diseases that were common and often lethal only 50 years ago are now rare in developed countries and some diseases such as smallpox have been eliminated worldwide. However, new diseases are continually cropping up, for which we may have no cure and, perhaps, no effective treatment. Aids is one of the most widespread of the new ones but even well-known diseases such as influenza are continually appearing in new forms.

The fact is that viruses and bacteria are able to change and evolve very rapidly, so we may always be catching up. Many of the diseases of the past originated with our farm or domestic animals (see Diamond, 1997) and new ones are still resulting from the transfer of infectious organisms from animals to man, as with influenza in Hong Kong, which apparently derived from poultry. So research will always be needed and progress may be very slow, as in the case of cancer.

Increasingly, alternatives to the use of animals are being found and this must be the aim. Some of these alternatives may involve the *in vitro* culture of human tissues such as skin or even organs, developments which are also not without their opponents.

A recent publication (UFAW/FRAME, 1998) provides a practical guide to those contemplating animal experimentation and wishing to explore all alternative options.

The arguments for the use of animals in medical research can be summarized as follows:

- Animals are the only appropriate, available models for treatment of humans.
- Development of new drugs, treatments and, especially, surgical procedures depends upon it.

- Medical research and advance depend upon using animals to understand animal physiology etc.

The arguments against the use of animals in medical research can be summarized as follows:

- Such experiments involve cruelty and poor welfare.
- Animals should not be reared simply to provide organs, tissues, antibodies etc.
- The use of animals is unnecessary and, whilst permitted, reduces the need and incentive to develop alternatives.
- Large numbers (millions according to figures on Home Office statistics although no accurate records are kept) of animals bred for scientific experiments in the UK are slaughtered because they are 'not quite right' for the tests. Animals included are monkeys, horses, dogs, cats, guinea pigs, mice and rats.

In addition, animals may be used in medical practice. Organs from animals (often pigs) have been used for a long time to replace defective human organs such as heart valves and this raises the possibility of animals being reared and grown just for this purpose. Not everyone likes the idea but does this differ from producing animals for food, hides and other products?

Somewhat different problems arise, however, when animals are specially bred for their susceptibility to disease or are genetically-modified (transgenic animals) so that they actually develop diseases like cancer. These techniques obviously make the animal more useful for some types of research and it can be argued that fewer animals are thereby needed, but many people reject the whole idea of deliberately producing an animal that will suffer in some way. Is this worse than rearing a normal animal that is then deliberately infected with the disease to be studied? Is either of them sufficiently comparable to a human being with the same condition for the results to be relevant?

If research is not done this way, what is the alternative? Is it all right to try out some possible new treatment for the first time on a human being suffering from the disease with no knowledge of how the treatment affects any living thing?

One of the problems with using animals to produce organs for transplanting into humans is that the animals have to be killed, although this is not necessarily at an earlier age than would be the case in food production. In some cases, however, the animals can produce medically-useful substances whilst living normal lives.

The transgenic sheep (Polly and Molly), produced at the Roslin Research Institute, yield milk containing human versions of the clotting Factor IX. Webster (1994) has pointed out that the milk containing ∝-1-antitrypsin from a single, genetically engineered sheep could keep 20 sick children alive at a cost of £50 per year, whereas with existing technology it would cost £10,000 to support a single child. The value of such animals virtually guarantees that they will be extremely well looked after, so there is unlikely to be a welfare problem in these cases (see Box 8.1). The welfare concerns relate to how the sheep is produced and the failures and losses of animals on the way. But if such animals can be cloned, it may not be necessary to go through this process repeatedly.

Box 8.1 *The Welfare of Valuable Animals*

The argument that medically-useful farm animals would be likely to be well looked after parallels that for valuable racehorses as opposed to horses for slaughter. However, this may only apply to some aspects of welfare. Racehorses can be cruelly ridden and show-jumpers can be excessively tested or exposed to unsuitable environments.

Producing very valuable products is not enough to ensure good welfare. Elephants and rhinos are cruelly killed for tusks and horns, horses have been ill-kept in Canada to produce Pregnant Mare Serum (PMS) and bears have been grossly ill-treated in China to 'milk' their bile. Some of these may be valuable products but their production is not dependent on good welfare; on the contrary, harvesting them may involve very bad welfare.

It is possible to envisage breeding flocks whose progeny are all able to produce the same substances in their milk. It now looks as though it will soon be possible to clone cattle that can produce valuable drugs in their milk (so-called 'pharming'), with the enormous advantage of the much greater milk yields that cattle can give.

These possibilities have raised great hopes and great fears and decisions are being made about how far research and developments arising from them should be allowed. Whatever control may be exercised in one country, it may be impossible to prevent less regulated development in other countries and difficult choices have to be made. The action required at the present time is to ensure that balanced, informed public debate occurs and that political decisions are not completely swayed by unconsidered, emotional reactions. The problems of coordinating international action have already been mentioned and the advantage of retailers in bringing about change across the world pointed out.

It is claimed that the potential advantages of the production of human proteins in the milk of transgenic sheep, goats and cattle and the production of organs for xenotransplantation are considerable (see Chapter 9).

Animals in Food Production

In addition to encouraging the retailers in raising standards, it is important to press for international agreement (this is even more true for wild animals, especially those that range widely, like whales and migratory birds). In agriculture, the reform of the Common Agricultural Policy (CAP) and WTO negotiations require action.

Reform of the Common Agricultural Policy

It is widely recognized that the CAP is in need of urgent and radical reform. This represents a great opportunity to obtain a better deal for animals. Compassion in World Farming (CIWF) and WSPA have produced a report on this very subject (Winter, Fry and Carruthers, 1997). They list 29 recommendations, which in summary are that:

- animal welfare should be recognized as central to CAP policy;
- schemes to facilitate less extensive livestock farming and to encourage better welfare should be reviewed;
- financial support should be on an area and not a headage basis; and
- training of farmers and stockpersons should be adopted.

The RSPCA and Eurogroup for Animal Welfare in their report (1997) also saw CAP reform as a major opportunity and recommended:

- decoupling payments which encourage intensive production;
- phasing out quota payments;
- linking payments to good welfare practices; and the
- withdrawal of refunds for the export of live animals (CIWF and WSPA made the same point, specifically for cattle).

They also proposed that priority (during the UK Presidency, January–June, 1998) should be given to:

- the phasing out of battery cages for laying hens;
- the adoption of the Directive on the Protection of Animals for Farming Purposes (Proposal COM(92)192 final – approved by the European Parliament in 1992);
- withdrawal of refunds for live exports of cattle; and
- incorporating European Parliament amendments into the regulation on organic livestock.

WTO Renegotiation

The next round of WTO negotiations will aim to reduce the percentage of farmers' income that comes from subsidy and to reduce intervention prices. Currently, the percentage of national farm income derived from a subsidy varies from less than 5 per cent (New Zealand) to about 50 per cent in the EU and 80 per cent in Japan. Unfortunately, as we have already seen, the initial discussions in Seattle in 1999 made very little progress.

Another area that is particularly in need of international attention relates to wild animals.

Wild Animals

The RSPCA/Eurogroup for Animal Welfare priorities include:

- Commission recommendations on the control of welfare standards in zoos should be changed to the much stronger form of a directive;
- phasing out pelagic driftnets (very damaging to dolphins and leatherback turtles, for example); and
- amending the Council Directive (79/409/EEC) on the conservation of wild birds to incorporate 31 January as the end date for all hunting seasons for migratory birds.

There is still need for international action on driftnets, better control of the killing of cetaceans and seals and of trapping methods.

Currently, some of the most controversial debates are about hunting and badger culling, both of which are concerned with pest control problems in relation to farm livestock production.

Hunting

Hunting is actually a much wider subject than fox- and stag-hunting, which is how it tends to be thought about in the UK.

Even fox hunting occurs on a wider scale in other countries. Britain has only four deer hunts compared with about 60 in France but about 200 packs of foxhounds (there are many more in Australia, New Zealand, Italy, Portugal and the USA). For example, the South China Tiger is being hunted to extinction for its body parts and it is estimated that there are only about 25 left alive in the wild. On the other hand springbok, kudu, eland, oryx and ostriches are being bred in a large private reserve in South Africa and the surplus animals are shot by people who pay to do it, the money helping to pay for the upkeep of the reserve. And there are others like it, where virtually all the big game such as antelope, giraffes, lions, buffalo and even old rhinos are available. That is not to say that all the money always goes to the reserve or to the local people, but the principle is the same. Where the local people do benefit, they have an interest in the animals and poaching can be more readily controlled. There are human ethical issues involved but the only welfare issue really relates to whether the killing and the method of hunting are humane.

Similarly, for fox- and stag-hunting, there are human ethical issues: many people are strongly opposed to killing for pleasure, so a case has to be made that it is necessary in order to control pests or growing populations. However, hunting with horses and hounds, as opposed to stalking, involves at least two welfare issues, the pursuit and the method of killing. Paradoxically, deer – although a prey species – appear to suffer greatly from a prolonged chase, whilst foxes – naturally predators – seem better able to cope. However, strongly opposing views are held by different groups of people, other than those that hunt versus those that do not.

There is also a view that there are better ways of controlling species: deer for example are more easily killed cleanly by shooting, and ten times as many foxes are shot by farmers in Britain than are killed by hunts. Others point out that there are also worse ways such as poison and trapping that might be used. Another view is that the numbers of animals are so few, relatively, that there are much more important welfare targets to focus on.

As pointed out earlier, it matters not at all to the animal whether it is the only one or one of thousands, and the animal neither knows nor cares why it is being hunted. However, numbers of animals involved may lend perspective to the issue. For example, it is estimated that in Great Britain there are 240,000 adult foxes producing annually about 425,000 cubs: gamekeepers kill 70–80,000, fox hunts about 16,000 and the majority die in road accidents.

Scientific evidence is scarce, but the Bateson Report (1996) concluded that deer suffer greatly during pursuit. This was based on a study, in which members of the Exmoor & Quantock stag hunts cooperated, of deer chased by hounds (for an average distance of 20km over about three hours) and then shot. The physiological effects were startling. After about 15km, the deer had used up all their glycogen (the energy store), muscle enzymes leaked into the blood and, at the end of the chase, the animals were completely exhausted. It is assumed that the 50 per cent that escape the hunt may be in a similar condition. However, Bateson's results have been challenged by several scientists (Poole, 1999), notably by a Joint Universities study on deer hunting, published in 1999, which criticized both his methods and conclusions. Subsequent studies by Harris and Wise (Aldhous, 1998) found relatively little muscle damage and concluded that the welfare problems had been greatly exaggerated. The debate continues.

No comparable studies have yet been carried out on the fox, but it does not follow that the results on deer apply to rural foxes, which naturally range over large distances in search of prey.

In addition to the social, economic and environmental consequences of banning hunting there are three main kinds of welfare consequences:

1   Clearly, the foxes would initially benefit from no longer being hunted.
2   It is argued that there would be welfare disbenefits to the fox because alternative methods of control would be worse.
3   Consequences to the horses and hounds. It is argued that large numbers of horses and hounds would no longer be required and

many would have to be destroyed. The numbers are substantial. It is estimated that about 95,000 horses (in Britain) are kept by the 16,700 people who hunt regularly and 37,000 of these are kept solely for hunting: between 15,000 and 20,000 might be slaughtered (see also Chapter 4). In addition, it has been estimated that some 12,000 hounds might be slaughtered. It is also argued that drag-hunts could replace live hunts, thus reducing the numbers of animals having to be destroyed.

When considering consequences, it must be remembered that some of them may not be inevitable: better options may be developed – and perhaps should be.

Action is being considered in the UK on both hunting and badger culling, as this is being written, and both issues divide people quite sharply. Probably the greatest need is to listen to the other side or, if genuinely in the middle, to both sides. Unfortunately, many people feel so strongly about such matters that they have relatively closed minds and are not really interested in the views of others. It is probably a great test of the maturity of a society and its citizens to be able to debate contentious, emotionally-laden subjects calmly and with some recognition that the other side are not actually evil. If we cannot debate rationally, we end up with confrontation and no possibility of an agreed way forward. Then, either strength, of one kind or another, will prevail or decisions are left to someone else.

A major factor in all of this is that responsibilities are less clear when wild animals are involved than is the case for domestic animals, whether farm livestock, pets, companions, animals for work or entertainment. A common requirement across most of these issues is identification (see later).

However, it is important to distinguish between the need to control pests, often related to conservation or the protection of other animals, and the methods used in control.

In Australia, for example, it is argued that kangaroos need to be culled because their increasing numbers threaten the fragile environment in which they live and the many other native species it sustains. The culling is currently on a substantial scale (over three million kangaroos from a population of more than 50 million of the four main species) and is claimed to prevent millions from dying of thirst and starvation during Australia's frequent droughts. The culling is carried out by licensed professional shooters and is strictly controlled.

In Scotland, it has been reported (Hart-Davis, 1997) that poor control of deer populations is resulting in the destruction of forests. But there is a further concern that inter-breeding may occur between native red hinds and sika stags originating from the Far East. It is feared that this could lead to loss of distinct species. This is a similar case to that in Spain, resulting from the importation of the aggressive Ruddy Duck from Carolina which now threatens the White-headed Duck by inter-breeding. The UK Government has just decided to try and eliminate the Ruddy Duck by shooting.

In Zoos

The UK is one of only five countries in the EU with laws designed to protect captive animals. There is much cruelty in other European zoos (the RSPCA found cruelty in Spain, Italy, France, Holland and Belgium). The RSPCA report (1988) is being considered by the EU Environment Council and it is hoped that controls will be introduced throughout the EU.

Those who go to zoos could exert enormous influence, by only going to those zoos that maintain high welfare standards or by expressing their views to the management, since it is their custom that zoos depend on for their income.

In Circuses

The report by Creamer and Phillips (1998), referred to in Chapter 5, made a recommendation for the UK that circuses should come under the Zoo Licensing Act (1981), which would immediately transform the conditions under which circus animals are kept during the winter months.

As with zoos, those who attend circuses could exert great pressure for improvement, by making their views known, joining pressure groups or by simply patronizing only those with high welfare standards, and, further, encourage the development of circuses without animals.

Identification of Animals

The problem of stray dogs and cats is easier to solve if each individual is unambiguously identified, and implanted devices that can be read externally, combined with a central register, are arguably the best way forward. Yet, in the UK, less than seven per cent of dogs are registered.

Recovery of stolen animals and fraud, tracing origins of disease, for example in farm livestock, and establishing responsibility for an animal, all require identification. For many years, cattle and sheep have been ear-tagged or ear-notched, cattle and horses have been branded or tattooed, dogs and cats have worn collars, but all these methods have disadvantages, including some concerning welfare, as in the case of ear-tags being torn out on fences.

Regulation of Ownership

The extent to which all animals that are owned should be identified and registered ought to be considered. Such a system would, of course, identify the owner. Should anyone be allowed to be an owner? Of any kind of animal? Or should ownership be regulated in some way? The clearest cases are where people have been convicted of cruelty to animals: should they be banned from keeping such animals, or any animals? In the UK, the courts can impose bans but this rarely happens.

For livestock farmers, there are proposals that individuals should be registered or licensed. If they were found to be unfit in any way, they could be de-registered or their licences revoked. This, it is argued, would be a powerful incentive to operate to high welfare standards but, like any offence, failure would have to be detected and the cost of inspection would have to be borne. Application fees might cover the costs of initial inspection but there is the further problem of regular monitoring and the powers required to inspect with or without notice.

In general, those concerned primarily with animal welfare favour some form of licensing and the balance of opinion amongst UK farmers could move in the same direction – not because they believe that it is necessary for them, or even for the majority, but to protect their industry from the minority who can so easily bring it into disrepute.

What about pets? Should the same arguments apply? Some countries do have dog licences, of course, as the UK did until 1988; and Reykjavik, in Iceland, banned the keeping of dogs altogether.

What about snakes and other exotic pets? In the UK, there has been a huge boom in the sale of exotic pets, including snakes, scorpions and tarantulas, many of which escape and are difficult to recapture. Often, they are deliberately dumped by people going on holiday or who can no longer afford to feed them. Some of these pets are poisonous and extremely dangerous, so the responsibility of the owner ought to be considerable.

Pet shops (under the Pet Shops Act of 1951) do not need to have specialist knowledge of the pets they sell, so they cannot necessarily give advice to customers, many of whom are not aware that they need it. Such shops require a licence but this relates to the posing of a health hazard to the public. Customers do not need a licence if the animal is non-venomous, but they do not even have to produce their licence (under the Dangerous Wild Animals Act, 1976) when they purchase venomous snakes, such as cobras.

As in most of these cases, education is needed and responsibilities should be recognized, but legislation may be needed to underpin all this and deal with those who are, for one reason or another, irresponsible.

Legislation

As described earlier, there are now major barriers to any one country simply passing laws to control animal welfare. The main one is the general requirement to allow free trade, worldwide and within blocks of nations, such as the EU. There is no direct interference with national legislation but its effect may be to affect the competitiveness of operators, producers and businesses within that country. The agreements on free trade then mean that no country can prevent importation from countries not constrained by the same legislation. This applies as much to regulation of experimental animals (the experiments can be done in another, less regulated part of the world) as to farm livestock (where cheaper food products can be imported from another country with much worse animal welfare standards).

The Treaty of Rome defined farm animals as 'agricultural products' along with vegetables etc. However, the Treaty of Amsterdam came into effect on 1 May 1999, and requires Member States to 'pay full regard to the welfare requirements'. This is a major step forward.

Ultimately, the ideal would be legislation that was everywhere based on common standards. This cannot be achieved quickly or across the board but it is possible, even worldwide, in certain areas.

World Issues of Animal Welfare

It is worth campaigning hard for improvements on a world basis where the problems are easily identified, where it is clear what changes should be made and agreement is feasible. Such agreement will be easier to achieve between major blocks of countries and this can only happen if there is agreement within a block, such as the EU for example.

Progress in Europe

Although the EU is a major trading block, it is embedded in a wider continent and in proximity to other nations wishing to join the community. So it is worth thinking about progress in Europe as a whole, even if it is initiated in the EU.

Table 6.1 listed the bodies within Europe that are responsible for advising the relevant ministers in different countries. It is not always the same (or similar) ministers or ministries, depending on the nature of the Council, but there is no reason why we should not aim to make it the same advice. It could transform the often political nature of the animal welfare debate in Europe, especially in the EU, if all ministers received, simultaneously, the same advice. There would then be a predisposition for ministers to agree and the likelihood of consequent action would be greatly increased and the process speeded up. As a starting point, there is no reason why the existing advisory councils should not liaise more closely and collaborate where appropriate. There is usually quite wide agreement across the scientific community involved, as to what constitutes good or bad welfare for any particular animal. Currently, the national councils vary in their coverage and it would be preferable that all covered all species.

With limited resources, it makes sense for each council to know about and make use of studies done by others. This could lead to agreement on recommendations or, at least, identification of the areas where such agreement was possible. European action could concentrate on such areas, in order to make early progress.

But I can see no reason why we should not go much further and faster and establish a European animal welfare council with a remit to advise EU ministers about animal welfare matters. Such a council would be best funded by the Commission itself and the members could be the chairs and secretaries of the national councils, and, as a first step, such a council could be formed informally by the voluntary agreement of the constituent bodies. Its existence would ensure liaison and encourage collaboration and could coordinate research programmes, all without any adverse effects on the existing national councils or erosion of their independence. Indeed, it would make it possible for national councils to work more cost effectively and within the European context in which their recommendations have to be implemented.

The UK Position

The UK does not have an advisory council dealing with all animals: it has a Farm Animal Welfare Council; an Animal Procedures Committee (APC) covering laboratory and experimental animals – though not specifically their welfare; a Companion Animal Welfare Council which was launched in 1999, and there are bodies coordinating the welfare interest of zoos.

For a European animal welfare council to develop, the UK itself would need to form a new body in one of two ways.

1   Government could set up an animal welfare council, with membership based on the chairs and secretaries of FAWC, APC, CAWC and other appropriate bodies. Meetings could rotate round the facilities of each member and a combined secretariat could be formed from those already existing. Costs and bureaucracy would therefore be minimal and none of the constituent bodies would lose any of their current freedoms, functions or independence.

2   An independent body could be established by a free association of the relevant constituent bodies, along exactly the same lines as above.

The functions of the new body could be:

- to liaise with Europe and, indeed, other countries;
- to ensure liaison between its own members and to identify over-laps and gaps;
- to encourage and guide the development of appropriate bodies to cover identified gaps;
- to consider and develop the ethical basis on which our attitudes to all animal welfare should be based. Banner (1995) recommended the establishment of an advisory standing committee to consider 'the broad ethical questions relating to current and future developments in the use of animals'. This was not accepted by the government but the Roslin Institute have suggested that the decision could be usefully reconsidered;
- to publicize the work of its members and to encourage informed public debate on animal welfare issues.

Only a small proportion of the public can realistically be involved in the improvement of animal welfare, other than in their individual behaviour and their support of active organizations. For the rest, the important thing is that they should know that the whole range of problems is being monitored by authoritative, independent bodies which can advise government on what needs to be done in their own country and liaise with relevant bodies in other countries to achieve international agreement on the best ways forward.

Progress in the Rest of the World

There are many organizations across the world working to improve the lot of animals, and linkages between them are facilitated by WSPA. But there needs to be greater recognition at the level of the UN and other world agencies. And ultimately there need to be agreed world standards of animal welfare. This may seem ambitious and may take a long time but it is important to aim high and believe that achievement is possible.

Summary

1 Awareness that there are problems is a first requirement and education has a major role in this.

2   Adequate information is then required, about the problem and about possible solutions.
3   The action needed will vary according to whether the problem involves an individual animal, a whole industry, international trade, professional bodies, cultural or religious practices, or new scientific developments.
4   Legislation is not always the best way forward but may be needed to provide a minimum 'safety net'.
5   Persuasion and education are necessary, especially in areas where legislation is impractical or ineffective.
6   We are all consumers, however, and, in total, have enormous economic power to bring about change.

9

Future Welfare Issues

'We cannot predict the future: we can do better than that – we can invent it' (Dennis Gabor)

It is natural, when thinking about the future, to focus on new developments that may give rise to new welfare problems or a changing pattern of priorities for dealing with them. But it is important to remember that most current welfare problems will remain for a long time and, on a world basis, on a massive scale.

Progress can often only be made slowly, partly because public opinion may change only slowly, partly because it nearly always takes time to implement improvements and partly because agreement on what constitutes an improvement and how best to implement it is only achieved very gradually. However, there are also encouraging examples of very rapid change, especially in the elimination of cruelty in specific cases.

Improvements, by definition, differ from what happens currently, and bringing about change may involve limiting people's freedoms. An optimistic view would hold that some problems will diminish, mainly because of changes in public opinion, focused by pressure groups or expressed through purchasing behaviour. These positive changes should include fewer animals being used in laboratories, zoos, circuses, rituals and festivals and fewer animals being hunted, except as part of necessary culling operations. This is mainly because the justification for many of these uses is slight and increasingly perceived to be so. The rate at which such change occurs will depend on many things but, in the case of laboratory use in medical research, will be most affected by the availability of adequate alternatives.

Some future problems may follow events over which we have no control. Global warming, for example, might result in natural disasters involving destruction of wildlife, but it might also result in injured animals and destroyed habitats. However, it is already clear in South-East Asia for example that fires started by people can get grossly out of hand and cause disaster on the same scale.

There may also be consequences of human activity that could be foreseen but seem not to be: animal protection is one example.

Animal Protection

As the world becomes more ecologically-minded and conscious of the importance of biodiversity, it must be expected that more species will be protected. The effect of protection will usually include an increase in the numbers of the protected species: at least this is a foreseeable possibility.

In some cases, this will result in the species becoming damaging pests. Current examples are geese damaging scarce grass on farmers' fields, tigers in India, elephants in Africa, apes on the rock of Gibraltar, and badgers in lowland England, where they are suspected of spreading bovine tuberculosis (TB) (see Krebs, 1997).

In the case of large and dangerous animals there may be a real case of conflict between people and animals, and the people affected are likely to be poor and relatively helpless. Furthermore, there may be no easy way of controlling population size. In the absence of natural predators, the old and diseased animals may linger on, but without greatly affecting either their food supply or the reproductive rate of the population. But culling the surplus fit animals has to be done with great care.

Elephants, for example, live in complex societal groups, with an age and sex structure that is of great importance, both to the elephants and to people in the area. Adult females may be the main contributors to population increase but they are also the key to disciplined and orderly behaviour of the young.

Moving animals to another area – which cannot go on indefinitely – suffers from the same difficulty of choosing which animals to move.

It is usually accepted that preserving a species involves preserving its habitat, but it may be that this has to include other species that control their rate of increase: even large and fierce animals are vulnerable when very young.

It goes without saying that culling to control population size should be undertaken as humanely as possible. Sometimes it is sensible to combine it with 'sport' in order to gain the resources necessary to sustain and regulate animal populations. In the case of big game, resources are required to protect animals from poaching.

Pest Control

Vertebrate pests are controlled in a variety of ways and, very often, this causes little concern. Rats, for example, have well developed nervous systems but receive little sympathy: they may be killed by dogs, by traps, by guns or by poison.

Government-approved poisons (eg anticoagulants such as Warfarin, Klerat, Ratak and Storm) are used to kill rats, mice, squirrels and moles. They may cause prolonged severe pain and distress to an estimated 20 million small mammals each year (Sainsbury et al, 1995). The issue of poisoning may receive greater public attention in the future should it increase, if other methods of control are banned. In some cases, poisons are specially developed to control a particular species. For example, in Australia, FST-2 has been designed to kill feral cats that are destroying species such as the eastern barred bandicoot, the numbat and the burrowing bettong.

New Sports Based on Animals

There is little sign that new sports will be developed that pose new risks to animal welfare, but there is an increasing awareness of some of the unintended consequences of existing sports. Angling in the UK, for example, was estimated in 1983 to result in the deaths of swans and ducks, due to the ingestion of lead shot; this included 8000 mallard. Entanglement in fishing nets in European waters (though not strictly 'sport') was estimated in 1995 to kill 10,000 to 100,000 marine mammals and diving birds. So it is possible that other unintended consequences flow from sports, existing or new, that do not themselves directly cause animal welfare problems.

Within existing sports, future welfare problems are most likely to be associated with the endless search for higher performance in domesticated animals, especially horses and dogs. This may be sought by feeding, training or, most probably, by breeding.

The last certainly carries some risks, since it may be obtained, for example, by selecting horses which are vulnerable to respiratory stress or leg-bone weakness. The first may lead to bleeding from the lungs and the second to bone breakage (also influenced by training methods).

Farm Livestock

The search for higher performance is even more general in farm livestock, where traditional breeding has always sought for higher performance in the form of higher milk yields per cow, more eggs per hen, higher prolificacy in breeding females and higher growth rate in meat animals.

The reasons are mainly related to feed conversion efficiency (FCE) (see Box 9.1). In addition to breeding, drugs and control of daylength have been used, and these products and processes will no doubt continue to be developed. Bovine somatotrophin (BST) is a relatively recent example of a method of increasing milk yields (see Box 9.2).

If farmers do not pursue efficiency, their competitors – both home and abroad – will be able to produce food more cheaply and low food prices are obviously attractive to consumers, even if the food is imported from afar with all the fuel usage and pollution that that implies.

Traditional breeding is now being reinforced by genetic modification and transgenics and it is in these areas that major welfare worries are likely. These technologies allow not only the genetic combination of species that would not normally interbreed, but the insertion of a single, selected gene from one species into another. The resulting offspring are unlike anything that has existed before and therefore pose questions about long-term consequences that cannot be answered in the short-term. Furthermore, it may be possible to replicate any particular outcome by cloning.

Box 9.1 *Feed Conversion Efficiency*

Many of the costs of keeping a farm animal are much the same, whether it is productive or not, and the expenditure on feed represents 50 to 80 per cent of the total cost. This is like an overhead cost which has to be spread over the resulting production, so the higher that is, the greater the economic efficiency.

The 'maintenance' requirement (ie the food needed to sustain the animal's functions, without anything for the output of meat, eggs or milk) is related to bodyweight, so that a large animal eats more and has to produce more than a small one. But, whatever the animal, doubling the output only increases the food needed for that output; it does not increase the maintenance requirement.

So economic and biological efficiency are both increased if a hen produces more eggs, a cow produces more milk, a ewe produces more lambs or a bullock grows faster. Hence there is a tendency for farmers to boost the individual productivity of their animals by better feeding and by selective breeding.

Box 9.2 *Bovine somatotrophin*

Bovine somatotrophin is a hormone that occurs naturally in the milk of cows and can be injected to increase milk yields.

There are, of course, arguments about whether it is safe, needed or justified, but the worries about the welfare of the cow are chiefly that:

- its use may increase the incidence of diseases and disorders, such as mastitis;
- continual injections may adversely affect welfare, for example at the site of the injection;
- adverse effects on welfare may only become evident over a long period of time.

The possible welfare concerns associated with embryo transfer (ET) are as follows:

- Methods have changed over the years, away from surgery (in cattle but not in sheep, goats and deer).
- Flushing embryos from the uterus requires skill and without it may result in damage to the lining of the womb.
- Embryo implantation is also an exact procedure and there are risks of pain, suffering and long-term harmful effects.
- If ET involves implantation of beef-type calves into dairy cows, difficult calvings can result. (This problem may also result from implantation of clones.)

Welfare is not an issue during the laboratory processes involved in cloning but may be so when clones are implanted in surrogate mothers. For example, many cloned calves are currently abnormally large at birth. The cloned animals themselves may be more likely to abort or die.

Similar techniques will make possible entirely new uses for farm livestock, for example in producing compounds for use in human medicine (see Table 9.1) and organs for transplantation into human beings.

Xenotransplantation

Xenotransplantation or Xenografting is the practice of transplanting tissue or organs from one species into individuals of a different species.

Pigs are currently being developed whose organs would be suitable for transplanting into humans, as it is already difficult to meet the demand from human sources, especially for hearts, kidneys, lungs and livers. It is argued that the pig will feel no different, will be more valuable and therefore better looked after and is little different from one kept for meat.

The whole subject is being subjected to close scrutiny, mainly because of the risk of transmitting animal infections (especially viruses) to humans receiving transplants and the fear that this could then infect other humans. (Not that organs from cadavers are necessarily free from such risks.) This might lead to the production of even more specialized animals (eg virus-free) but it is not foreseeable exactly how this might be achieved.

Table 9.1 *Medically-useful Compounds that can be Produced by Animals, Genetically Engineered and Cloned*

Animal	Compound	Treatment
Sheep and goats	1 Factor IX	For the treatment of haemophilia
	2 ∝-1-antitrypsin	To treat cystic fibrosis
	3 Human fibrinogen and Factor VII	To promote blood-clotting
	4 Human Factor VIII	To promote blood-clotting
	5 Human antithrombin III	Blood plasma protein for accident victims
Cattle	Human Growth Hormone	To treat dwarfism and AIDS-related illnesses
	Beta-interferon	For multiple sclerosis
	Human serum albumin	Use in blood transfusions

Note: The process for deriving compounds for medical use from genetically engineered and cloned animals is known as 'pharming'.

In 1996, a UK Department of Health Advisory Group on the Ethics of Xenotransplantation (Kennedy, 1997) recommended that 'it would be ethically unacceptable to use primates as source animals for xenotransplantation, not least because they would be exposed to too much suffering'. This report distinguished between the possibly-justified use of primates in research, because this might benefit large numbers of people, from primates used as sources of organs for actual transplantation, where one primate would only benefit a few.

The welfare concerns, which are mostly focused on pigs as the animals most likely to be used, include the effects of genetic modification; the removal and replacement of eggs from sows under anaesthesia; hysterectomy and removal of piglets from the sow; and serial tissue sampling to test for infectious agents for example. The report stated that serial or sequential removal of tissue, other than for such sampling, would be ethically unacceptable.

The Government agreed in 1997 to set up a national committee to oversee xenotransplantation and announced the establishment of the United Kingdom Xenotransplantation Interim Regulatory Authority (UKXIRA).

Artificial Insemination

New developments may involve not new techniques but their applications to different animals. One example of this is artificial insemination (AI).

Artificial insemination involves the interruption of the natural process and the collection of the ejaculated semen for examination, dilution and possibly storage. The majority of UK dairy cattle are artificially inseminated and the main advantages are:

- No male need be kept at all on some farms, and bulls are often large, dangerous animals.
- Genetic improvement can be accelerated. In cattle, a single ejaculate can be used to inseminate 20 to 200 females: in this way the influence of a superior male can be rapidly passed on to the next generation.
- New genes can be introduced to a pig herd, for example, without the attendant risk of disease which may be imported when buying a boar.

However, there are concerns that AI in turkeys, for example, has allowed the production of very heavy males, where natural insemination is no longer possible because the males are now too heavy and their claws could damage the females' backs, and AI might be extended in sheep by direct introduction of sperm into the womb through the abdominal wall, by surgical intervention.

Organic farming

Other developments, involving changes in the patterns of food consumption, may also have large effects on the number of animals farmed. For example, there could be increases in organic farming that would affect both the numbers of animals and the ways in which they are kept.

It is often not realized that organic farming includes strict rules to protect animal welfare. It is, however, commonly recognized that organic farming systems rely on crop rotations, crop residues, animal manures and legumes in order to maintain fertility and this imposes upper limits on the stocking rates of livestock that can be supported.

It is part of the organic philosophy that these lower stocking rates will help to limit diseases due to parasites and that the generally lower levels of individual animal performance will lessen the incidence of metabolic disorders.

Where these measures fail, it is a requirement, at least in the UK, that animals should not suffer and must therefore receive appropriate veterinary treatment, even if they thereby lose their organic status. Any significant increase in organic farming should therefore improve animal welfare and result in more extensive systems of animal husbandry.

Vegetarianism

Vegetarianism involves a reduction in the consumption of animal products. Vegetarians eat no meat but they may continue to consume milk, eggs, butter, cheese and other milk products. Vegans consume no products of animal origin. It has been established that, in the UK, 4 to 5 per cent are vegetarians, a further 6.5 per cent eat no red meat and less than 0.005 per cent are vegans.

Many countries are encouraging greater consumption of fruit and vegetables and a reduced consumption of meat. The net effect is to reduce the total number of farm animals required. It is therefore possible that either land will be farmed more extensively or that intensive livestock keeping will continue but with less animals. However, in developing countries, increasing affluence is generally accompanied by increased consumption of animal products, so the world picture may be very different from the projections considered here.

Increasing Demand for Animal Products

In world terms the biggest development is likely to be a vast increase in the numbers of animals kept for food in developing countries. It is predicted (Delgado et al, 1999) that by 2020 developing countries will consume 100 million tonnes more meat and 223 million tonnes more milk than they did in 1993. Developed country increases are predicted to be 18 million tonnes for each product. These projections require the production of 292 million tonnes more cereals and have other implications for the land and feed required. Certainly all the existing welfare problems associated with farm animals would be greatly magnified by the sheer numbers involved.

The reason for predicting such increases is the steadily increasing demand for animal food products in developing countries. Currently, people in developed countries obtain on average 27 per cent of their energy and 56 per cent of their protein from animal food products. The comparable figures for developing countries are 11 per cent and 26 per cent respectively. Population growth will further increase the likely demand.

Rabbits, Ostriches and Emus

Some new welfare problems will be associated with the use of species not commonly associated with agriculture, at least in the UK. Rabbits have been eaten for centuries and there is a substantial world trade in rabbit meat, but they are not normally thought of in the UK as farm livestock. The UK produces about 1500 tonnes of rabbit meat per year; Europe produces about 250,000 tonnes. The high reproductive rate of rabbits and their lean meat, however, may give high feed conversion efficiency, provided that diseases can be adequately controlled. But they are also susceptible to battery-style production methods using controlled lighting and their needs for privacy and nesting material, for example, may be important in achieving high welfare standards. Similar concerns would then apply to rabbits as are very evident in relation to battery hens (see Chapter 4).

Ostrich farming has been carried out for some time in South Africa and there has been increasing interest, both in the UK and worldwide, in the farming of both ostriches and emus. Welfare concerns are of two kinds. Firstly, ostriches are relatively wild and need a great deal of space, but the same economic considerations that apply to all other classes of farm livestock will also apply to ostriches and there may be a tendency to overstock or otherwise restrict space.

Secondly, little is yet known about the effects of British winter weather on these essentially hot climate birds, although the Universities Federation for Animal Welfare (UFAW) has funded a study of this and recommend that ostriches should have access to adequate shelter and more concentrate rations during the winter.

In recent years, ostriches have been identified as a promising new enterprise in New Zealand, where it has been calculated that they are four to five times as efficient as sheep at converting grass to meat. (Five thousand breeding hens have the potential to produce 100,000 offspring, with the potential to produce one million birds.)

New Animal Feedstuffs

Animal feedstuffs are constantly changing to meet nutritional needs and to respond to the price of ingredients. It may seem unlikely that they will give rise to major welfare concerns, unless by virtue of additives or supplements; but bovine spongiform encephalopathy (BSE) may have resulted from changes to the way feedstuffs were processed.

However, there have been suggestions that gene transfer could produce 'grazing' pigs or poultry, by enabling them to produce their own enzyme – cellulase – for digesting fibre. As Webster (1994) has pointed out, this is unlikely to work, because the alimentary tracts of these animals are not designed to retain fibre long enough for such digestion to occur.

New Farming Methods

Quite apart from the developments already referred to, some simple features of farming can have adverse or beneficial effects on welfare. For example, in Scotland, hundreds of capercaillie and thousands of other grouse are killed each year when they fly into fences erected to protect trees from deer. Simply hanging strips of orange netting on the fences can greatly reduce the number of collisions. In Hampshire, a farmer has made a cow path of sand and wood shavings, parallel to the previously used concrete road on which flints occur, and enormously reduced lameness, which is one of the major welfare problems in dairy cows, and also greatly reduced the time the cows take to come in and out for milking. The speed at which cows are driven may be crucial: cows place their feet with great care.

Pets

The desire to keep something different or even dangerous may have many motives but it also may have many unintended consequences. Veterinary surgeons are increasingly having to learn how to treat injured or sick species that are unusual: this must involve costs of training and treatment, but, provided that owners are prepared to pay the costs, the capacity to deal with such animals will undoubtedly develop to meet the need.

Already, in the UK, the numbers of vets specializing in small animal practice greatly exceed those dealing with horses and farm livestock. It has long been known that pets are an important source of pleasure and companionship for the very young and the very old but their importance for disadvantaged and disabled people has emerged more recently. Riding for the disabled has been particularly successful and can positively help people to do things that are otherwise impossible for them, creating confidence and increasing their quality of life.

Many pets are thus actually useful, in calming people by reducing blood pressure for example, in guiding the blind and the deaf and alerting epileptic sufferers to impending attacks. But these developments do not generally involve exotic pets (with some exceptions, such as Capuchin monkeys – see Chapter 5): on the contrary, they depend mainly on animals like dogs and horses, which are well-known and well-understood, easily trainable and not too difficult to look after. This does not mean that they are immune to welfare problems, although the uses just described are less likely to give rise to cruelty or neglect. As described in Chapter 4, common pets do give rise to massive welfare problems, some of them due to ignorance about how to look after them.

This kind of ignorance seems likely to be even worse with exotic pets, especially as they may be essentially wild species, unused to confinement or human contact. The welfare problems of exotic pets are, in fact, to an even larger extent due to a lack of understanding of their needs, but the best of modern pet superstores do give advice and supply the specialist equipment that may be needed. However, the numbers involved are unlikely to be anything like as great as those of dogs and cats.

What is more likely in the future is that new knowledge may require changes in the way we keep some common pets. For example, it has recently been found that gerbils separated from their mates become depressed, socially withdrawn and have altered sleep patterns. Yet such animals may be kept on their own in order to avoid fighting or mating. Hamsters, by contrast, are normally solitary, but may prefer company, even if this involves fighting, to being kept alone in bleak, unfurnished cages.

Sadly, with the improvement in nutrition of pets brought about by the ready availability of balanced pet foods, diseases of excess are increasing. The main ones are obesity, diabetes and a range of dental conditions.

As mentioned earlier, some current problems will continue and could get worse, such as the overproduction of dogs, purely for profit, by uncaring breeders who sell to a public often quite ignorant of their needs.

Another welfare problem associated with pets has been caused, in the rabies-free UK, by the quarantine laws, which required all dogs and cats entering this country to spend six months in quarantine, separated from their owners. In 1995, 5394 dogs and 4126 cats were committed to quarantine in the UK and, from 1972 to 1996, 2500 out of 170,000 animals in quarantine died, but none from rabies. For the first time, in 1996, one case of bat rabies was recorded in the UK. Other countries, such as Sweden and Norway, which are also rabies-free, successfully introduced a vaccine-based system in May, 1994, and New Zealand now simply restricts dogs and cats to the owner's home for 30 days. Such a scheme has now been introduced in the UK, and the first dog to enter under it did so on 28 February 2000.

The RSPCA and others have been pressing for passports for dogs and cats, based on vaccination, blood-testing and permanent identi-fication (see Box 9.3) and it has recently been agreed that by 2001 a passport scheme will operate in most European countries. The scheme will cover the EU, Monaco, Andorra, the Vatican, Liechten-stein and Switzerland, as well as rabies-free islands such as New Zealand, Japan, Barbados, Jamaica and Australia.

Animals Used in Experimentation

As mentioned at the beginning of this chapter, it is to be expected that the number of experimental animals – at least in the EU – will diminish, partly because of public opinion leading to consumer pressure and partly because alternatives are steadily being developed.

A common target for criticism is the use of animals in cosmetics testing and some firms now advertise their products as not having been tested on animals (some, however, are using ingredients tested on animals by others). The Dutch have gone furthest in legislation against any animal experiment which may also be achieved by other means, and the British Government announced an end to animal testing of cosmetics in 1997.

But it is estimated that fewer than 300 animals were so used in 1996, compared, for example, with some 20,000 rodents sacrificed

Box 9.3 *Passports for Pets*

Passports for Pets is a UK organization lobbying Parliament for an alternative to quarantine for dogs and cats entering the country. The present system is criticized as being unnecessary and cruel: unnecessary because no case of rabies has been found in the 200,000 dogs and cats quarantined over the last 25 years (including 3000 that died and were subjected to brain examination); cruel because the animals are kept in concrete-floored cages with little exercise or human companionship.

It is argued that alternatives such as vaccination (with an inactivated vaccine), antibody tests to check level of protection, secure identification and, where necessary, a six-month delay to guard against pre-incubation are available and all can be recorded in a passport. Some animals such as those failing the tests would, however, still need to be quarantined.

In September 1998 the British Government proposed a scheme that would allow dogs and cats to enter the UK from EU and other selected countries without six months quarantine, provided that those countries were free from rabies, the animals were fitted with identification microchips and were accompanied by health certificates issued by vets (the so-called passports). Methods of vaccination are steadily improving but generally require 30 days or more for immunity to develop. It must be remembered, however, that rabies is a very serious disease, killing more than 40,000 people per year worldwide, and it is feared that, if entry is made easier, vastly more animals will be involved than the current number.

in the production of antibodies, some of them involving the growth of tumours in mice. Such monoclonal antibodies can now be produced by tissue culture and this should greatly reduce the numbers of animals used.

Many rats and mice are reared solely to generate tissue for experiments; they are not themselves used for experiments but killed for their tissues. In the UK, it is estimated that 14 per cent of animals used in research are bred for their tissues. However, it appears that human tissue could be used as an alternative; this has been proposed by the antivivisection group Animal Aid and this practical focus is an encouraging sign, as opposed to protest alone.

An encouraging sign of a constructive dialogue in this area in the UK was the establishment in 1992 of the so-called 'Boyd' group, whose 30 members include representatives of research organizations, animal welfare groups and some animal rights groups (Matfield, 1996b). The purpose of the Group is:

> *'to explore and promote dialogue on issues of common concern related to the use of animals in science, to clarify where there is consensus and where there is disagreement; and to recommend practical steps towards achieving agreed goals.'*

Subsequently, in 1996, the first European Congress on the Ethics of Animal Experimentation was held in Brussels. In Australia and New Zealand, there are regular meetings of the Australia and New Zealand Council for the Care of Animals in Research and Teaching (ANZCCART).

Another area in which animals are used is in military research. Here, too, it is to be hoped that the numbers will be steadily reduced. There are some encouraging signs. For example, the US Army Medical Research Institute of Chemical Defense (USAMRICD) has deliberately reduced the number of animals used over the last 11 years by 92 per cent and has adopted the Three Rs, of Replacement, Reduction and Refinement, as a guide.

Reduction in the numbers of animals used is a possibility in all research. For example, transgenic sheep that can produce Factor IX in their milk could be replaced by a smaller number of cows. Currently, the world need (3–5kg annually) would require 50 to 100 sheep. It has been pointed out that a single cow carrying the gene for human serum albumin, which is used in blood transfusions, could produce 80kg a year in its milk (currently worth about £150,000). Similarly, one cow could produce 10kg of growth hormone, reducing the cost by a factor of thousands.

However, the costs of purification are not included and there are similar risks of virus transfer as mentioned in relation to xeno-transplantation.

The Development of Alternatives to the Use of Animals in Experimentation

In 1992, it was reported that some of the most expensive drugs, such as the human growth hormone at £400,000 per kg, and the blood clotting agent Factor VIII at £700,000 per kg, could be produced much more cheaply from bacteria by genetic engineering. Other alternatives include the use of slime mould, cultured rabbit cells, frog spawn, maggots, fruit flies (with human genes inserted), potatoes and complex computer programmes to better understand what controls cell division.

However, many scientists believe that animal experimentation will remain necessary for some medical research for some time and in 1991 the British Association issued a 'Declaration on Animals in Medical Research', stating that 'Continued research involving animals is essential for the conquest of many unsolved medical problems such as cancer, AIDS, other infectious diseases, and genetic, developmental, neurological and psychiatric conditions.' The Declaration also said that alternatives should be used wherever possible and, where essential, animals should be treated humanely.

Amateur Care of Wild Animals

Whilst the RSPCA (UK) takes in about 20,000 wild animals that are injured or otherwise in need of care each year, there may be as many as one million such animals looked after by non-professionals. The latter may not be very successful and in a recent survey by the RSPCA (Australia) some 34 per cent of the animals were dead within five days, a further 25 per cent within 25 days and seven per cent between 25 and 100 days. Only about six per cent were released into the wild, with unknown success.

Amateur carers are actually licensed in Australia, though not in the UK, which illustrates the fact that, although it would seem like a good idea, it may be ineffective without monitoring – and who would do this and who would pay for it? Carers are well-intentioned and are often only responding to people bringing them casualties, or those thought to be casualties. Very often animals such as fox cubs or deer calves are picked up because it is thought that they have been abandoned, when it would be better to leave them where the mother can find them again.

So what can be done? If the carers were not there, there is no possibility of the relevant professional organizations taking on the sheer numbers of animals involved. Advice and education may be one answer, but perhaps the professionals could organize a scheme that actually involved the amateur carers. This problem may increase with the growth of public interest in wildlife and illustrates the limits of control by regulation.

Regulation

Most people manage to object to what they see as over-regulation in their lives, whilst calling for more control and regulation over the activities of others.

A common reaction to most of the welfare issues described in this book is of this kind: there should be a law against it or the law should be more rigorously enforced.

Naturally, farmers rarely take this view of farm livestock, pet-keepers would be against it for most pets, hunters want freedom for their country pursuits, users of experimental animals do not want their laudable aims constrained and sportsmen, circus-owners and zoo-keepers believe that they know best how to deal with their animals.

Hence, it is my central theme that solutions to welfare problems are best sought through wide consultation and may well involve several different activities including advice, education, registration, licensing, voluntary codes of practice, regulation and legislation. We should only be interested in effective solutions and this involves considering all the consequences of proposed actions: they cannot be arrived at by focusing narrowly on the welfare problem itself.

Thinking About the Future

The idea of at least thinking about problems that may arise in the future seems sensible, but the track record for any kind of forecasting is very poor and any account is likely to be coloured by personal views and experience. Nevertheless, it is important to encourage everyone concerned about animal welfare to give some thought to the ways in which future problems may arise.

There is probably no short- or medium-term prospect of major reductions in the use of animals in the service of man. It is a salutary thought that modern methods of warfare have virtually eliminated the use of animals on the battlefield and thus enormously reduced the suffering endured in the past – mainly by horses. Even so, new military uses for animals such as dolphins are still being devised. Large numbers of animals will continue to be farmed and increasing numbers 'pharmed', but there is no good reason why their welfare should not be protected.

It may be that modern technology will also displace guide-dogs, sniffer dogs and all those animals kept currently to perform a service – often with apparent enjoyment. But pets and recreational animals such as ponies are a different matter. The stresses of modern life, the increasing numbers of old people and those living alone, and increasing concern about the special needs of disadvantaged people all suggest that the numbers of pets are likely to increase. This reinforces the argument presented in Chapter 8 that the welfare needs of pets should receive more attention.

Summary

1 Future welfare issues will include, unfortunately, a great many of the current problems, which will remain for a long time, worldwide, on a massive scale.
2 Areas of increasing concern will include disease and pest control in the interests of other animals, conservation, and human health and safety.
3 New problems are likely to be associated with the search for ever-increasing levels of animal performance in agriculture, medicine and sport, and an ever-growing interest in exotic pets.
4 Amongst the positive trends, which will need constant encouragement, is the development of effective alternatives to the use of animals in medicine and work.

10

Reflections, Unifying Themes and Conclusions

'The worst sin towards our fellow creatures is not to hate them but to be indifferent to them: that's the essence of inhumanity' (George Bernard Shaw)

Reflections

I set out with fairly clear notions as to why I wanted to write this book but, during the course of its preparation, a number of things have become clear to me that were either vague before or not even in my mind at all.

This is due partly to the need to think in an integrated way about the welfare problems of such a wide range of animals and partly because I have had to confront the sheer scale of these problems worldwide. One's feelings of pity and revulsion at the enormity of the problems are repeatedly stirred up on reading seemingly endless, vivid accounts of animal suffering and the brutality, ignorance, callousness and cruelty that cause it.

The impact of facing up to cruelty and suffering on this scale can be almost unbearably depressing and may have a paralysing effect apparent in the sad reflection 'what can I or anybody possibly do about such a massive problem?'

There is so much wrong and yet it is not always clear how on earth one could put it right. Rules and regulations may be needed but cannot cover all needs and there is always resistance to further regulation. So much depends upon the attitudes and behaviour of millions of individuals, in different cultures in different countries at different stages of development. This paralysing effect is exacerbated by confronting problems in detail but, even then, we can only be aware of a tiny sample.

However, it is important to recognize that this situation is not unique to animal welfare. It would be exactly the same if one was confronting the world picture for human suffering, cruelty, poverty or injustice. The totality is appalling, apparently beyond remedy and yet we cannot accept that nothing can be done.

It is probably a mistake to see such matters as problems with neat solutions. In most cases, the situation is very complex and there is no solution. We need to determine the right direction in which to move and then to move as fast as is possible in the circumstances.

It is understandable that many people feel unable to cope with the total scene and, in animal welfare, confine their concerns to one species or another. This also makes practical sense, since it is hardly possible to support all the campaigning organizations, or for one person to make a difference on such a broad front. But it does risk getting things out of proportion and is a poor basis for judging priorities between competing claims on our attention. One of the reasons for a book covering all kinds of animals was to provide a perspective against which any specific problem could be seen.

Equally, reviewing the vast number of people and organizations working hard and effectively to improve the lot of animals, of all kinds and in all parts of the world, demonstrates that much is being done and much more is possible.

Keeping Things in Perspective

The idea of keeping a sense of proportion and being reasonable makes obvious sense but is often misused. As George Bernard Shaw said, 'Progress is not made by *reasonable* men', and in many circumstances one has to behave unreasonably in order to achieve change. Otherwise, as was pointed out earlier, no one takes any notice. Being unreasonable, however, is not the same as behaving unlawfully.

Clearly, the fact that there are relatively few circus animals does not make cruelty to any of them any more tolerable. But the sheer scale of livestock farming does mean that any welfare problem may be greatly magnified. Similarly, poaching for ivory or rhino horn seems worse if it occurs on a large scale and the deaths of illegally imported pets are more horrifying because of the numbers.

Individuals matter, even if not many are involved, but small numbers may be due to accident, carelessness or ignorance. Large numbers cannot be excused in these ways: they are likely to be the result of quite deliberate action or failure to act. Similarly, the scale of a problem does affect the resources and effort needed to put it right and, since resources are nearly always limited, difficult choices have to be made and priorities selected.

This is one of the reasons why many solutions have to be used. Legislation and regulation may be needed but are not always either effective or cost-effective. Education may be the best long-term answer in some cases, but it does not always have to be long-term. Persuasion, pressure of public opinion and peer group or consumer power all have their place in bringing about change for the better.

There is no point in banning something, for example, if it does not actually improve the welfare of animals. The consequences of action, however well-intentioned, have to be thought through and this may require wide consultation and expert advice. That is why it was argued in Chapter 5 that science has a role in deciding what to do about a welfare problem – even if the initial concern is largely and rightly emotional. This is especially so in cases where there is public demand for 'something to be done about it' but the public are not really competent to say what that should be. However, the science has to be disinterested, objective, independent and relevant.

Of course, it is neither possible nor desirable to understand or even be aware of the total scene in detail: indeed the totality of animal suffering is unknown and unknowable in detail. But there are some common themes and principles which only become apparent when a very wide view is taken. Furthermore, the wider view does often illuminate or even change the way in which we look at the areas with which we are most familiar. For example, many pet-keepers look with different eyes at their rabbits, hamsters and gerbils, having considered the problems of zoo animals.

Each of us may look with horror and incomprehension at practices accepted and taken for granted in other countries. Even within Europe, there are deep-seated differences in attitudes to eating horses, methods of slaughter and the use of animals in sport. Across the world, attitudes vary with regard to the eating of dogs, the control of strays and the hunting of big game.

Those who work with laboratory and experimental animals tend to see them differently from those not involved and workers in livestock markets and abattoirs may get accustomed to habits that others find objectionable.

The outsider's view is frequently different, though not necessarily right. Considering the welfare problems of animals other than the ones that one is personally involved with can often be very illuminating. This is true for physical treatment but perhaps even more so for psychological aspects.

It is easy to underestimate the intelligence and feelings of animals, but appreciation has been increasing steadily and most people now appear to credit whales and elephants, for example, with both. In the UK, dogs and horses have long been held to be intelligent and able to understand much of what is said and with feelings quite easily hurt, but people very closely involved with other animals, such as budgerigars, cats, pigs and even snakes, may also regard them in much the same way.

We tend to attribute these qualities more readily to warm-blooded, furry animals which are capable of facial expression (so important in human assessments), and of which birds and reptiles are hardly capable. Curiously enough, this is not always so for very cuddly animals such as small dogs, rabbits and kittens, which are often treated rather like toys, with no minds of their own but objects of pampering.

We also underestimate the ability of animals to communicate with each other, sometimes because we cannot interpret their sounds, as for example with complex bird song, sometimes because we cannot hear them, as for example the very low frequency sounds of whales, elephants and crocodiles, and sometimes because we are not aware of the means being employed, as for example the colour changes in fish and sonar in dolphins.

A more surprising failure on our part is our inability to appreciate their need to communicate. We have gradually become aware of the importance of social structure in animal communities and, recently, the importance of life-long relationships even to gerbils and their acute depression when separated from their mates. Yet many pets are kept alone, amid a general ignorance of their social needs. Very commonly, animals are provided with little of interest in their immediate environment and no stimulus to thought, feeling or action. It is relevant to note that Sweden is just enacting a law that bans the keeping of single pets.

All these are small illustrations of deficiencies in our attitudes to animals which may be revealed to us by thinking about the problems and needs of other animals than the ones we are used to.

However, my main reason for attempting an integrated account of welfare across all the relevant animal species was to see whether general principles emerged that would serve as a general guide to welfare, its definition, problems, needs, measures and improvement. Such general principles are likely to be based on identified common ground, so I have tried to identify unifying themes that represent this.

Unifying Themes

The reason for describing these general principles of animal welfare is that, although we may not yet be able to state them in a completely satisfactory form, such that they can be applied to all sentient animals, whatever the species and wherever they are kept, it is important to establish that a useful start can be made. But it is clear that what ought eventually to emerge from the unifying themes – the themes that seem to be common for at least all the kinds of animals considered here – is a general basis for progress in improving animal welfare. In spite of the complexity of the issues, these themes, I believe, strongly reinforce the view that progress is actually achievable and worthwhile beyond doubt. There is a logical sequence of questions within which such themes may be found. For reasons of clarity we can divide the subject of our enquiry into two groups – animals that are kept, and those that are not kept but are affected by human behaviour. For each group a distinct series of questions needs to be constructed:

Animals that are kept

1   How are the animals obtained and how should they be?
2   How are the animals kept and how should they be?
3   How are they used, treated or trained and how should they be?
4   How are they finally disposed of?

5 Who is responsible for 1–4 and to whom are they accountable?
6 What regulatory controls should apply to animal owners and keepers, in terms of qualification and competence?

Animals that are not kept but are affected by human behaviour

1 (a) Are they deliberately affected and is this acceptable?
  (b) If so (ie 'yes' to both parts), what are the consequent responsibilities?
2 What controls should apply in relation to competence?
3 If they are affected only as a consequence of some other activity, what are the consequent responsibilities?

It goes without saying that all the answers to these questions must satisfy the relevant legal requirements, both national and international. But this, of course, only provides a minimum, and often inadequate, safety net. Good animal welfare will also go beyond what the law requires. Since each question will probably turn out to be complex and generate secondary questions, we cannot assume that there will be neat answers and, if there are, that we can currently make authoritative, simple statements about them. But it is worth trying and a start can be made by identifying the elements that must be embodied in each answer.

Unifying Themes for Animals that are Kept

Obtaining the Animals
Animals may be caught, bought, bred or found. Wild animals clearly have to be caught and, if they are then kept, it is as pets, for exhibition in zoos and menageries, conservation or, possibly, for the production of medicinal substances such as snake venom. It is hard to see the justification for catching wild animals in order to keep them as pets or for exhibition. For conservation, keeping wild animals permanently would have to be justified on the grounds that only in this way could a species be saved and that those kept would be bred for progeny that would be subsequently released in a proper and controlled way. Animals caught for relocation only come into the category of those 'kept' because it may not be feasible to transport them and release them immediately.

Animals that are acquired by purchase should only be bought from properly approved dealers, known to operate to high welfare standards in the whole of their business, and should not normally include wild species. Obtaining animals bred by other people comes into this same category. Breeding from one's own animals only raises special welfare problems if they derive from the breeding methods employed.

The control of reproduction is a major feature of domestication and breeding has to be subject to control of timing and frequency, for good reasons. But the methods of insemination, whether natural or artificial, of controlling ovulation and prolificacy, for example by the use of hormones, and inducing birth, may all need to be considered from a welfare point of view. However, breeding, in the widest sense, includes the choice of parents and the selection of offspring.

In agriculture and sport, animals are bred for ever-higher performance, but for pets and showing in which animals are bred for show points, fashion and novelty, quite extreme shapes often result, with the final version being different from the original and not infrequently physically or physiologically damaged or vulnerable to injury and disorder. Dogs are a spectacular example, where the extraordinary range of size, shape and weight found in current breeds has been derived from a common (wolf) ancestor entirely by traditional methods of breeding. Bulldogs that have impaired breathing and breeds susceptible to hip dysplasia are obvious examples of unsatisfactory outcomes. But goldfish, cats, pigeons, fancy fowl and many others may also exhibit gross distortions of the original species.

Finally, wild animals may be found injured or abandoned, and it may not be possible to return them to the wild. They should not be prevented from doing so but they might not be able to survive if they did.

The keeping of animals
The Five Freedoms of the FAWC represent a good starting point, but they were formulated with farm livestock in mind, so the following is a list of the needs that have to be met for all animals that are kept, whatever the purpose.

- *Space* – area, volume and all dimensions needed to express essential behaviour patterns;

- *Features for needs and stimulus* – nest-boxes, perches, swimming water, climbing facilities, bedding, hidden food, balls, soil, mud, sticks;
- *Light* – intensity, wavelength, sunlight, light/dark patterns, shade;
- *Temperature* – range, daily and seasonal;
- *Protection* – from predators, parasites, adverse weather, sun, wind, draughts, excessive noise, bullying, disease and injury, ill-treatment;
- *Food supply* – quantity, quality, safety, nature and form, digestibility, nutritional balance, fibre, major and minor elements, supplements;
- *Water supply* – quantity, quality, temperature, availability;
- *Companionship* – sufficient contact with other animals, mainly of the same species.

It is easy to see that, even if these cover the needs of all types of animal, more detailed specifications can only be stated in relation to a particular animal type. In principle, however, they represent a checklist, every item of which has to be satisfied for every animal kept. Furthermore, if the details given are incomplete, the framework can be further clothed from practical experience or new scientific knowledge.

The Use of Animals

How animals are used is a question that covers their treatment whilst being kept but also the ways in which they are transported, sold, marketed, exhibited, trained, handled, loaded and unloaded, moved about, restrained, and treated for disease control or prevention, and for routine operations, such as castration and tailing. Many of these activities cannot satisfy the needs expressed in the previous section but the same checklist is nonetheless relevant. Adequate space, for example, is still necessary in transport, at markets and in shops, even if the actual amount is less than required for continuous or permanent occupation. Food, water, protection and comfort all have to be considered in all these circumstances but there are some additional criteria to be met.

Training not only has to avoid cruelty and physical suffering but psychological suffering as well. Exhibiting animals has to protect the animals' need for privacy but also protect their integrity and dignity. When being handled, animals are especially vulnerable to human impatience and irritation, either because of the numbers involved, the large size and stubbornness of animals or their small size and the sheer difficulty of catching them.

In all of this, equipment design plays a big part. Steep or slippery loading ramps, badly designed collecting pens and races, small cage openings and an atmosphere of panic can all exacerbate the problems of handling. Restraints include collars and leads, tethers, muzzles, holding crates and crushes. No restraints should cause suffering and most should be used only for very short periods. Identification tags and collars may have to be exceptions, however.

The Disposal of Animals

Ultimately, the disposal of animals means death by one means or another. There are three important and rather separate issues here:

1   The method of slaughter/euthanasia must be appropriate to the species and size of animal. The same methods are not appropriate for all.
2   The restraint used during killing should minimize suffering and fear.
3   The procedure preceding death should be as calm, orderly and as free from suffering as possible.

Animals injured in accidents may have to be put down on the spot and horses severely injured in racing are commonly shot on the course. Speed is probably the most important of the controllable factors in such cases. The disposal of dead bodies raises no animal welfare problems.

Responsibility for Animal Welfare

It is essential, in the interests of animal welfare, that all aspects of the responsibility for the animal are clearly defined so that someone can be held accountable. In most cases, it is the owner, but very often others are actually in charge and responsibility is delegated. This may be the case, for example, with drivers of transport vehicles, people riding or exercising other people's animals and people providing grazing for other people's animals. It is vital that, where possible, written contracts make clear where responsibilities lie and that, in any event, this is made clear to all concerned.

It should not be possible to shed responsibility by abandoning an animal or to claim ignorance as to where the responsibility lies.

Identification of individual animals is a vital part of this, although this turns out to be a rather more complex matter than at first appears.

Regulations for Animal Welfare

It is clearly desirable that anyone having a responsibility for an animal should be competent to discharge that responsibility.

This may require some sharing of responsibility in the case of young children and others under training or instruction but the ultimate responsibility cannot be shared. Competence should relate to whatever the responsibility entails, whether it is for feeding, moving, treating, training, housing, herding, exercising, slaughtering or selling. In many cases, there are regulations about the competence required and the need to demonstrate this by qualifications or certification of attendance at relevant courses.

Some activities, for example, may only be undertaken by a qualified veterinary surgeon or certified slaughterman. Ownership of some animals, such as dogs or dangerous animals, may require a licence. This may involve inspection of premises and facilities or may simply supply a sanction such as loss of licence, for example, for certain offences.

Some sectors such as riding establishments may operate their own registration schemes, so that users can choose whether to patronize regulated or unregulated organizations.

One of the most powerful effects on public opinion is where people are convicted of cruelty to animals and yet are allowed to continue to keep animals of the same kind. This is manifestly wrong and some means has to be found to prevent it. Licensing is one possible option.

Unifying Themes for Animals that are not Kept but are Affected by Human Behaviour

Animals that are not 'kept' are generally wild, but there are marginal cases. Ponies, for example, which are simply left on the moor and rounded up annually are not 'wild' species but are not really domesticated either. Bull-fighting and some game shooting are also somewhat borderline.

Wild Animals that are deliberately affected

Wild animals that are deliberately affected are mainly in the following categories:

- Hunting, shooting and fishing
- Culling
- Pest control
- Relocation.

Clearly, these may overlap, but this should not influence the outcome if general principles are the aim.

The main common ground is where the animals are killed. The welfare requirement is always that they should be killed as painlessly and quickly as possible. This should determine the method employed and it will vary with species and circumstances. Pest control, however, may not always involve killing but may use methods of 'scaring', as with bird scarers of all kinds, fencing (including electric fencing), guard dogs (for sheep) or chemical deterrents spread around valuable crops for example. None of these need pose welfare problems.

In the case of hunting, shooting and fishing, however, there may be an element of chase: indeed, the 'sport' may depend upon this being prolonged. Hunting (including whaling) may cover substantial distances, although bull-fighting, for example, might be regarded as prolonged hunting in a confined space (there is therefore no pretence that killing the animal is the only or even the main objective). Fishing may not involve killing but may include prolonged playing of the hooked fish, although this, it may be argued, is no more prolonged than is required to land a heavy fish only secured by a thin line. Shooting may be based on stalking rather than chasing and welfare depends largely on its accuracy and what happens to animals that are only wounded.

Chasing animals is bound to involve stress: the question is whether this is more than the animal is subjected to in its normal life, either because of the speed of the chase, its duration or the nature of the terrain it is forced to cover. Clearly, welfare is adversely affected if the chase goes beyond what is normal. In the case of the fox, as a predator it would not normally be chased at all, but it may nonetheless be accustomed to travelling long distances.

As has been repeatedly stated, the reasons why it is chased or killed are of no consequence to the animal: the welfare problems relate to the issues identified above. These reasons may raise ethical issues relating to human behaviour but that is a quite separate matter, although it has an important bearing on what society finds acceptable or tolerable.

Consequent responsibilities
If society finds an activity acceptable or tolerable, the welfare needs of the animal may still be met by humane killing and restricted chasing. This may be justified because of the importance of the pest control achieved or the destruction of a dangerous animal.

But some societies accept practices, such as bull-fighting and bear-baiting, that cannot possibly be carried out other than with outright cruelty. From an animal welfare point of view, they should be banned.

Controls
Whenever standards based on good animal welfare are agreed, there are always questions about monitoring, enforcement and sanctions, and whether any of these should have legal backing or rest on codes of best practice, voluntary or mandatory, as a condition of joining a particular association. In some cases, much depends upon the competence of those involved, including killing, whether in a slaughterhouse or by shooting in the field. Only certain weapons are allowed in any case (certain guns, for example, but not crossbows) but competence is not just a question of weapons expertise but shooting skills in the field. In many countries, slaughtermen are required to be licensed, as are the premises, but the latter is related mainly to food safety and hygiene. The subject of competence at least needs to be considered wherever people are responsible for animals. It may not be appropriate to control by licensing or registration but education and training may be needed.

Non-deliberate effects
Animals may be affected accidentally as part of unrelated activities, such as in road or boating accidents. If wild animals are killed in this way, that is the end of the matter for those involved, but preventive measures may be taken, such as underground passages for animals to avoid crossing roads, markers on overhead wires, signals associated with nets in marine fishing and warning signs for the public.

The most difficult problems occur with animals that are injured, the most common cases resulting from road accidents and pollution. In the case of road accidents, the result may not be known, unless the animal is large, such as a deer; and, of course, this is not confined to wild animals – horses, dogs, cats, cattle and sheep are commonly hit.

Oil pollution chiefly affects marine animals, including seals and sea-otters, but birds are usually the most numerous casualties. Not all species can be successfully cleaned but there is a natural human desire to try, even though the methods themselves may cause stress.

Conclusions

Having surveyed the nature and scale of the world's animal welfare problems, and identified what needs to be done and by whom, the overall conclusion to be drawn is that the citizen should be concerned about animal welfare.

The sheer numbers of animals involved in agriculture, as pets, in sport, entertainment, experimental procedures especially, are so enormous that even if the majority are well treated most of the time, the numbers actually suffering are also very large. There is thus an unacceptable amount of man-made suffering by direct cruelty or poor welfare in the world as a whole and probably in every country within it.

It is impracticable for every citizen to be actively concerned about – or even aware of – all of it and most citizens have many other pressing concerns. But it does mean that every citizen who keeps or affects an animal is able to contribute by ensuring that it does not suffer by reason of ignorance, neglect or active ill-treatment. This personal responsibility cannot be shrugged off with excuses about other worries or that there is nothing that an individual can do: for the most part, such responsibility is voluntarily acquired. But there are other things that every individual can do as part of their daily lives. It has been pointed out that almost everyone is a consumer of animal products or services that use animals and every consumer has the power to influence the ways in which those animals are treated. So individual action can actually be effective. Individual voices are rarely loud enough, however, and benefit greatly from being combined with others. Joining, participating or supporting an organization seeking to improve welfare not only provides a megaphone for the individual voice but provides expertise that the individual may lack and a means of taking effective actions beyond the individual's capacity.

The existence of large numbers of relevant organizations is not a reason for assuming that individuals need not do anything themselves: rather, they present opportunities for making one's own contribution vastly more effective. In addition, membership of, or support for, animal welfare organizations greatly extends the area over which an individual can make a difference. Such organizations can undertake campaigns and programmes in other parts of the world where, otherwise, an individual would have no influence at all.

So, although the problems are large and may often seem intractable, there is no reason to feel that the individual can make no difference, even though it must be accepted that, for many people, the scope may be rather limited. Furthermore, there are encouraging developments in many parts of the world, on the part of governments and local authorities, practitioners including farmers and others who keep or treat animals, retailers and in public opinion.

Even where an individual cannot be actively involved, support for others – even if only moral – is very important. Every citizen has some responsibility for the way members of society behave and for the ways in which animals are treated. Every citizen should care but, above all, none should be indifferent.

Summary

1   A broad view of the whole range of animal welfare problems is desirable but cannot be achieved by all citizens.
2   However, keeping things in perspective must not obscure the need for action wherever cruelty occurs or welfare can be improved: this also means wherever animals are kept, used, reared, transported, sold or slaughtered.
3   It is necessary to ensure that the people involved are accountable, and this means a clear location of responsibility.
4   Progress in animal welfare is actually achievable and all citizens have some responsibility, but individual actions are not enough.
5   The importance of organizations devoted to animal welfare cannot be overstated and they need support of all kinds.

Appendix 1

BFF & WSPA Recommendations

The recommendations are contained in the WSPA/BFF Zoo Report, Version 8c, *Wild Animals in Captivity*. The legislative programme of zoo reform is to be undertaken with the following objectives:

1 Establishing minimum standards for animal welfare on a global basis.
2 Reducing the number of captive animal facilities.
3 Ensuring that the closure of zoos does not cause unnecessary suffering of zoo animals.
4 Establishing as soon as possible operational and breeding licences embracing effective zoo management and the ability of staff to care for individual animal needs.
5 Establishing a 'passport system' for wild animals in zoos to ensure accountability in the transfer, sale and exchange or disposal of stock.
6 Providing for a 'Zoo Bond' in the form of a guaranteed closure fund into which all zoos pay and which underwrites operational and care costs during a specified period of closure (12 months has been suggested). This should be an essential part of forward planning in any attempts to reform and refine the global zoo industry if, as has been suggested, a major reduction in collections were to take place over the next 20 years or so.
7 Establishing a consultative panel including wildlife professionals, humane society representatives, zoo professionals and animal behaviourists and psychologists to draw up, as a matter of urgency, ethical guidelines, procedures and a code of conduct aimed at:

8   ensuring that the individual biological welfare of wild animals in captivity is addressed and meaningful minimums established;
9   ensuring that the environmental needs of wild animals in zoos are met and that clear minimums are established;
10 ensuring that the social needs of wild animals in zoos are considered fully and effectively responded to and that the Code of Conduct and its application becomes a statutory threshold against which the ability of a zoo to obtain an operating licence is set.

Appendix 2

The Major Animal Welfare Organizations

Ten thousand animal protection contacts can be found in the *World Animal Net Directory* (WAN, 1999) with links to more than 1200 web sites. The addresses of the World Animal Net are as follows:

Eastern Hemisphere:
World Animal Net
24 Barleyfields
Didcot, Oxon OX11 0BJ
United Kingdom
Tel: +44 (1235) 210 775
Fax: +44 (1235) 210 775
E-mail: worldanimalnet@yahoo.com

Western Hemisphere:
World Animal Net
19 Chestnut Square
Boston, MA 02130
United States
Tel: +1(617) 524 3670
Fax: +1(617) 524 1815
E-mail: worldanimalnet@yahoo.com
Web Site: http://www.worldanimal.net/
(World Animal Net Directory http://www.worldanimal.net/wan.htm)

It is not feasible to give details here of so many organizations and too much must not be read into the selection that follows. The largest are listed, but also some that cater for special groups of animals.

Adcovates for Animals 10 Queensferry Street, Edinburgh, Scotland EH2 4PG
Protection of animals from cruelty, prevention of the infliction of suffering and the abolition of vivisection.

Animal Health Trust (AHT) Lanwades Park, Kentford, Newmarket CB8 7UU
An independent veterinary research institute with a primary interest in horses and small animals.

Battersea Dogs Home 4 Battersea Park Road, London SW8 4AA
Rehoming of stray or unwanted dogs.

British Veterinary Association Welfare Foundation 7 Mansfield Street, London W1N 0AT
Promotion of animal welfare by supporting a wide range of projects and activities.

Compassion in World Farming Trust 5a Charles Street, Petersfield, Hampshire GU32 3EH
A major campaigning organization on behalf of farm animals.

People's Dispensary for Sick Animals (PDSA) Whitechapel Way, Priors Lee, Telford, Shropshire TF2 9PQ
Provision of free veterinary treatment for the animals of those who genuinely cannot afford it.

Royal Veterinary College Animal Care Trust (RVC ACT) Hawkshead Lane, North Mymms, Hatfield, Herts AL9 7TA
Exists to improve standards of veterinary care in its small animal and equine hospitals. Veterinary education.

Scottish Society for the Prevention of Cruelty to Animals (SSPCA) Braehead Mains, 603 Queensferry Road, Edinburgh, Scotland EH4 6EA
Has similar aims to the RSPCA (which does not operate in Scotland). Has an inspectorate, welfare centres, clinics and an ambulance service.

World Society for the Protection of Animals (WSPA)   2 Langley Lane, London SW8 1TJ
The World Society for the Protection of Animals aims to promote cooperation amongst animal protection societies internationally with the object of preventing cruelty to animals and relieving their suffering. It has over 300 members, including the major national organizations, and offices in the UK, US, Canada, Costa Rica, Colombia, Brazil and Kenya. It organizes major international campaigns and responds to disasters worldwide that affect animal welfare. Notable campaigns involve invoking informed public opinion against bullfighting, fur farming, export of dogs to Asia, dancing bears in India, Bulgaria and Serbia, bear baiting in Pakistan, inadequate housing of bears in Japanese bear parks and poor treatment of captive elephants in India and Sri Lanka.

Rescue missions following disasters have included Hurricanes George and Mitch, earthquakes in Colombia, military hostilities in Sierra Leone and the Balkans, for example, and fires involving orangutan in Indonesia and Malaysia.

RSPCA UK   Causeway, Horsham, West Sussex RH12 1HG
The RSPCA is the oldest and largest animal charity in the world, with an international, national, regional and branch organization, to prevent cruelty, promote kindness and alleviate suffering of animals. It focuses mainly on companion animals, horses and donkeys, food animals, laboratory animals, animals in the wild, in entertainment, sport and fashion, and in education. The RSPCA's Inspectorate is the largest animal welfare law-enforcement agency in the world, and the largest non-governmental law-enforcement agency in England and Wales. It operates an extensive network of general animal hospitals, wildlife hospitals, national and branch animal centres, clinics and an animal ambulance service.

RSPCA, Australia   PO Box E369, Kingston, ACT 2604, Australia
A federation of the eight Societies (state/territory) representing them nationally and internationally. To prevent cruelty to animals, operate clinics and inform public opinion.

Royal New Zealand Society for the Prevention of Cruelty to Animals Inc (RNZSPCA)   PO Box 15-349, New Lynn, Auckland, New Zealand
Has similar objectives to both the above and, like them, employs an inspectorate able to act where offences are identified.

Universities Federation for Animal Welfare (UFAW) The Old School, Brewhouse Hill, Wheathampstead, Herts AL4 8AN
An internationally respected animal welfare charity, promoting the welfare of all the animals we affect, education, research and training.

Blue Cross Shilton Road, Burford, OX18 4PF
Over 100 years old, has 11 adoption centres, three hospitals and one clinic, and two equine centres. Engaged in rehousing of pets, help to the animals whose owners cannot afford veterinary treatment, and education.

Humane Slaughter Association (HSA) The Old School, Brewhouse Lane, Wheathampstead, Herts AL4 8AN
Aims to improve the welfare of food animals, especially at slaughter, in abattoirs and markets. Engaged in education and the development of mobile slaughterhalls.

Eurogroup for Animal Welfare 13 rue Boduognat, 1040 Brussels, Belgium
Based in Brussels, this group links the principal animal protection organizations in the 15 European Union Member States. It makes representations to the Council of Ministers of the European Union.

The Humane Society of the United States (HSUS) 2100 L St, NW, Washington DC 20037, USA
Founded in 1954 to promote the humane treatment of animals, it is the largest animal-protection organization in the US, with nine regional offices. It is involved in animal protection, education, research and legislative action.

International Fund for Animal Welfare (IFAW) Warren Court, Park Road, Crowborough, East Sussex TN6 2GA) (Headquarters at 411 Main Street, Yarmouth Port, MA 02675, USA
Founded in 1969 to fight against the Canadian commercial seal hunt, now mainly focused on three major worldwide campaigns: Commercial Exploitation and Trade in Wild Animals, Habitat for Animals, and Animals in Crisis and Distress. Involved in emergency and disaster relief, sanctuaries and pet shelters.

The Massachusetts Society for the Prevention of Cruelty to Animals (MSPCA) 350 South Huntington Avenue, Boston, MA 02130, USA
Founded in 1868, runs eight animal shelters and three veterinary hospitals in Massachusetts, involved in rescue, education, publications and law enforcement.

Society for the Protection of Animals Abroad (SPANA) 15 Buckingham Gate, London SW1E 6CB
Treating animals, mainly in North Africa, for people who cannot afford private veterinary care.

National Canine Defence League 17 Wakley Street, London EC1V 7RQ
Exists to protect and defend all dogs from abuse, cruelty, abandonment or any form of mistreatment, both in the UK and abroad. Engaged in rescue, rehousing, education and advocacy.

New Zealand Foundation for the Study of the Welfare of Whales Massey University, Private Bag 11222, Palmerston North, New Zealand
Focuses on ways to prevent or reduce the suffering of whales and dolphins in natural disasters or through human activities.

Cats Protection 17 Kings Road, Horsham, West Sussex RH13 5PN
Primarily concerned with the rescue and rehousing of cats and is also involved in education and advice in Great Britain and Northern Ireland.

The Donkey Sanctuary Sidmouth, Devon EX10 0NU
Probably the largest of its kind in the world, it has taken into care over 7400 donkeys and publishes *The Professional Handbook of the Donkey* (Svendsen, 1997), which lists the addresses of 57 organizations concerned with donkey welfare, in over 20 countries. Its own mission statement is as follows:

> *'To prevent the suffering of donkeys in the UK and Ireland through the provision of high quality professional advice, training and support on donkey care and welfare and by providing permanent sanctuary to any donkey in need of refuge.'*

Also founded and run by Dr E D Svendsen MBE, is the *International Donkey Protection Trust,* with investigations in Kenya, Mexico and Ethiopia.

Donkeys in many developing countries are vital to poor people: yet in Ethiopia, for example, their life expectancy is nine years and in Mexico it is 16 years, whilst in the UK it is around 30 years. It has been demonstrated that five years can be added to the lower figures by simple parasite control and better feeding. This is in circumstances where the loss of a donkey can mean disaster to the weakest members of the family.

The British Horse Society (Welfare – Rescue) Stoneleigh Deer Park, Kenilworth, Warwickshire CV8 2XZ
Has an extensive network in the UK, with over 120 volunteers, working to improve the welfare of horses and ponies. Engaged in education and training, rescue and rehabilitation.

The International League for the Protection of Horses (ILPH) Anne Colvin House, Snetterton, Norwich, Norfolk NR16 2LR
For the worldwide protection and rehabilitation of horses.

Home of Rest for Horses Speen Farm, Slad Lane, Lacey Green, Princes Risborough, Buckinghamshire HP27 0PP
Looks after horses when they are discarded as unfit or too old for their original purposes.

References

AWAC (1998) *Code of Recommendations and Minimum Standards for the Welfare of Ostrich and Emu*, Animal Welfare Advisory Committee, Wellington, New Zealand

Aldhous, P (1998) 'The chase is on', *New Scientist*, 19 Sept, p5

Banner, M (1995) *Report of the Committee to Consider the Ethical Implications of Emerging Technologies in the Breeding of Farm Animals*, HMSO, London

Bateson, P (1996) *The Behavioural and Physiological Effects of Culling Red Deer*, Report to the Council of the National Trust, UK

Bateson, P (1992) 'Do animals feel pain?', *New Scientist*, 25 Apr 1992, pp30-33

Boydell, P and Crossley, D (1997) 'CT scanner: toy or tool?', *Practice*, Nov-Dec, pp572-574

Broom, D M (1992) 'Welfare and Conservation', in Ryder, R D (ed) *Animal Welfare and the Environment*, Duckworth in association with the RSPCA, Horsham

Burrell, I (1998) 'Animal smuggling is the most lucrative crime after drugs', *Independent*, London, 4 Aug 1998, p6

Camphuysen, C J, Duiven, P, Harris, M P and Leopold, M F (1997) *Sula*, vol 11, pp157-174

Canadian Federation of Humane Societies (1998) 'Humane Transport?' *Animal Welfare in Focus*, Spring 1998, p6

Carruthers, S P (ed) (1991) *Farm animals: it pays to be humane* CAS Paper 22, Centre for Agricultural Strategy, University of Reading

Carter, P and Rickard, K M (1998) 'Animal-based research - using animals for animals' benefit', in *Ethical approaches to animal-based science*, Proceedings of the Joint ANZCCART/NAEAC Conference held in Auckland, New Zealand, 19-20 Sept 1997, ANZCCART, New Zealand, pp145-146

Cooper, M E (1987) *An Introduction to Animal Law*, Academic Press, London

Creamer, J and Phillips, T (1998) *The Ugliest Show on Earth*, Animal Defenders, London

Dawkins, M S (1998) 'Animal Suffering – the Biobehavioural Background', in Michell, A R and Ewbank, R (eds) *Ethics, Welfare, Law and Market Forces: The Veterinary Interface*, Proceedings of a Royal College of Veterinary Surgeons and UFAW Symposium, pp1–11

Delgado, C, Rosegrant, M, Steinfeld, H, Ehui, S and Courbois, C (1999) *2020 Brief 61*, May 1999, International Food Policy Research Institute, Washington

Diamond, J (1997) *Guns, Germs, and Steel*, Norton, New York

DSPA (1996) *The Vulnerable Animal in Intensive Livestock Farming*, Thirteenth Report of the Study Committee on Intensive Farming, The Netherlands

Eason, C, Wickstrom, M, Milne, L, Warburton, B and Gregory, N (1998) 'Implications of animal welfare considerations for pest control research: the possum as a case study', in *Ethical approaches to animal-based science*, Proceedings of the Joint ANZCCART/NAEAC Conference held in Auckland, New Zealand, 19–20 Sept 1997, ANZCCART, New Zealand, pp125–130

Elson, A (1985) 'The economics of poultry welfare', in Wegner, R M (ed) *Second WSPA Symposium on Poultry Welfare*, Butterworth & Heinemann, Guildford

Eurogroup for Animal Welfare (1987) *Summary of Legislation Relative to Animal Welfare at the Levels of The European Economic Community and The Council of Europe*, Eurogroup for Animal Welfare, Brussels

Eurogroup for Animal Welfare (1988) *Analysis of major areas of concern for animal welfare in Europe*, Eurogroup for Animal Welfare, Brussels

European Commission (1997) 'The Welfare of Intensively Kept Pigs', Report of the EC Scientific Veterinary Committee, DocXXIV/B3/ScVC/0005/1997, EC, Brussels, 30 Sept, electronic publication

Ewbank, R (1999) 'Animal Welfare', in Ewbank, R, Kim-Madslien, F and Hart, C B (eds) *Management and Welfare of Farm Animals* (UFAW Farm Handbook, Fourth edition), UFAW, Wheathampstead, pp1–15

FAWC (1997) *Report on the Welfare of Laying Hens*, MAFF PB3321, London

Ford, B J (1999) *Sensitive Souls*, Little, Brown & Company, New York

Fox, N and Macdonald, H (1997) *Welfare Aspects of Killing or Capturing Wild Vertebrates in Britain*, Hawk Board

Fraser, A F and Broom, D M (1990) *Farm Animal Behaviour and Welfare*, CAB International, Wallingford

Gregory, N G and Lowe, T E (1999) *Expectations and Legal Requirements for Stunning and Slaughter in Slaughterhouses*, MIRINZ, Hamilton, New Zealand

Harrison, R (1964) *Animal Machines*, Vincent Stuart, London

Hart-Davis, D (1997) 'Red alert', *Independent*, London, 11 October 1997, p10

HMSO (1993) *Statistics on Scientific Procedures on Living Animals in Great Britain 1992*, Cm2356, HMSO, London

IUDZG/CBSG (IUCN/SSC) (1993) *The World Zoo Conservation Strategy: The Role of Zoos and Aquaria of the World in Global Conservation*, Chicago Zoological Society

Kennedy, I (1997) *Animal tissue into humans*, Advisory group on the Ethics of Xenotransplantation – A Report, HMSO, Norwich

Kestin, S C (1995) 'Welfare aspects of the slaughter of whales: Analysis and Interpretation of 1992 and 1993 humane killing data', *Animal Welfare*, vol 4, pp11–28

Kiley-Worthington, M (1990) 'The Training of Circus Animals', in *Animal Training*, UFAW, pp65–81

Kirkwood, J and Best, R (1998) 'Treatment and rehabilitation of wildlife casualties: legal and ethical aspects', in *Practice*, vol 20(4), pp214–216

Krebs, J R (1997) *Bovine Tuberculosis in Cattle and Badgers*, Report by The Independent Scientific Review Group, PB3423 MAFF, London

Laslett, D (1997) *Is Relocation the Solution to Overpopulation? – A case study of the Koalas of Kangaroo Island*, 1998 RSPCA Australia Scientific Seminar: Wildlife Rehabilitation and Relocation, Kingston

Levinger, I M (1995) *Shechita in the Light of the Year 2000*, Machon Maskil l'David, Jerusalem

Matfield, M (1996a) 'A short history of the three Rs', *RDS News*, October 1996, RDS UK, London, pp6–7

Matfield, M (1996b) 'Speaking with the enemy', *Science and Public Affairs*, Winter 1996, pp47–49

McInerney, J P (1994) 'Animal Welfare: An Economic Perspective', in *Valuing Farm Animal Welfare*, Proceedings of a Workshop held at the University of Reading, 30 Sept 1993, Bennet, R M, Occasional Paper no 3, Department of Agricultural Economics and Management, University of Reading

Mellor, D (1998) 'How can animal-based scientists demonstrate ethical integrity?' *Ethical approaches to animal-based science*, Proceedings of the Joint ANZCCART/NAEAC Conference held in Auckland, New Zealand, 19–20 Sept 1997, ANZCCART, New Zealand, pp19–31

Moore, G (1999) 'Ethical Review of Animal Experiments in the UK – an evolutionary process', *B&K Science Now,* vol 8, issue 1, Spring 1999, pp5-9

Pickering, D (1992) 'World agriculture', Chapter 3 in Spedding, C R W (ed) *Fream's Principles of Food and Agriculture*, Blackwell Scientific Publications, Oxford, pp45–93

Poole, RWF (1999) 'Banned by bad science', *Telegraph Weekend*, 2 October, p13

Reiss, M (ed) (1996) *Living Biology in Schools*, Institute of Biology, London

RSPCA and Eurogroup for Animal Welfare (1997) *Memorandum on animal welfare to the United Kingdom Presidency of the Council of the European Union*, RSPCA, Horsham

RSPCA (1988) *European zoos – behind the bars: The need for a European Directive*, RSPCA, Horsham

Sainsbury, AW, Bennett, PM and Kirkwood, JK (1995) 'The welfare of free-living wild animals in Europe: harm caused by human activities', *Animal Welfare*, vol 4, no 3, pp183–206

Spedding, C R W (1996) *Agriculture and the Citizen*, Chapman & Hall, London

Starkey, P (1995) *Animal Traction in South Africa: Empowering Rural Communities*, Development Bank of Southern Africa, Guateng

Starkey, P and Ndiamé, F (eds) (1986) *Animal Power in Farming Systems*, Friedr Vieweg & Sohn, Braunschweig

Stauffacher, M (1985) *Steuerung des agonistischen Verhaltens bei der Entwicklung einer tiergerechten Bodenhaltung für*

Hauskaninchen-Zuchtgruppen, Darmstadt-Kranichstein, KTBL-Schrift, 311, pp153-67

Stauffacher, M, (1992) 'Group housing and enrichment cages for breeding, fattening and laboratory rabbits', *Animal Welfare*, vol 1, pp105-25

Stevenson, P (1997) *Factory Farming and the Myth of Cheap Food,* Compassion in World Farming Trust Report, CIWF, Petersfield

Studbooks, *International Zoo Yearbook,* The Zoological Society of London, London, vol 31-32

Svendsen, E D (ed) (1997) *The Professional Handbook of the Donkey*, 3rd edn, Whittet Books, London

Travers, W (1993) *Wildlife Times*, vol 2, no 2, Born Free Foundation, pp12-13

UFAW (1990) *Animal Training*, Proceedings of a Symposium organized by UFAW, September 1989, Cambridge

UFAW/FRAME (1998) *Selection and Use of Replacement Methods in Animal Experimentation*, UFAW/FRAME, Wheathampstead

van Putten, G and Elshof, W J (1978) 'Observations on the effect of transport on the well-being and lean quality of slaughter pigs', *Animal Regulation Studies*, vol 1, pp247-71

WAN (1999) *International Directory of Animal Protection Societies*, de Kok, W (ed), World Animal Net Inc, Boston

Webster, J (1994) *Animal Welfare: A Cool Eye towards Eden*, Blackwell Science, Oxford

Wernham, C V, Peach, W J, and Browne, S J (1997) *British Trust for Ornithology Research Report* 186, Thetford, Norfolk

Wilkins, D (1992) 'Animal Welfare and the Environment: Are they always Compatible?', Chapter 8 in Ryder, R D (ed) *Animal Welfare and the Environment*, Duckworth (in association with the RSPCA), London, pp73-80

Winter, M, Fry, C and Carruthers, P (1997) *Farm Animal Welfare and the Common Agricultural Policy in Europe,* Compassion in World Farming Trust and World Society for the Protection of Animals Report, Oct 1997, CIWF, Petersfield

WSPA/BFF (1994) *Wild Animals in Captivity,* Zoo report, WSPA/Born Free Foundation, London/Dorking

Zinko, U, Jukes, N and Gericke, C (eds) (1997) *From guinea pig to computer mouse,* Euroniche, Leicester

Bibliography

General

Other publications consulted included the following:

Bowles, D (ed) *Agenda 2000 – The Future for Farm Animal Welfare in the European Union*, RSPCA Report, RSPCA, Horsham

Cobham Resource Consultants (1997) *Countryside Sports – Their Economic, Social and Conservation Significance*, Standing Conference on Countryside Sports, College of Estate Management, Reading

Eurogroup for Animal Welfare (1988*) Analysis of Major Areas of Concern for Animal Welfare in Europe*, Eurogroup for Animal Welfare, Brussels

Harrison, R (1998) *Farm Animal Welfare: What, if any, Progress?* The Hume Memorial Lecture, 26 November 1987, Royal Society of Medicine, London, UFAW, Wheathampstead

Lymbery, P (1997) *Beyond the Battery – A Welfare Charter for Laying Hens*, CIWF, Petersfield

MAFF CAP Review Group (1995) *European Agriculture – the Case for Radical Reform*, PB2279 MAFF, London

O'Brien, T (1995) *Gene Transfer and the Welfare of Farm Animals*, CIWF, Petersfield

O'Brien, T (ed) (1995) *Modern Breeding Technologies and the Welfare of Farm Animals*, a CIWF Report by d'Silva, J and Stevenson, P, CIWF, Petersfield

O'Brien, T (1998) *Factory Farming – The Global Threat*, CIWF, Petersfield

POST (1992) *The Use of Animals in Research, Development and Testing*, Parliamentary Office of Science and Technology Information Foundation, London

Roslin Institute (1997) *Annual Report 1996–97*, Roslin Institute, Edinburgh

Stevenson, P (1993) *The Welfare of Pigs, Cattle and Sheep at Slaughter*, CIWF, Petersfield

Stevenson, P (1995) *The Welfare of Broiler Chickens*, CIWF, Petersfield

Stevenson, P (1997) *Factory farming and the Myth of Cheap Food*, CIWF, Petersfield

Legislation

It is not possible to list the relevant legislation for all countries but the following are examples of what is available in the UK.

BSAS (1999) *Farm Animal Welfare – Who Writes the Rules?* Russel, A J F, Morgan, C A, Savory, C J, Appleby, M C and Lawrence, T L J (eds) Occasional Publication no 23, BSAS, Edinburgh

Cooper, M E (1987) *An Introduction to Animal Law*, Academic Press, London

Eurogroup for Animal Welfare (1987) *Summary of Legislation Relative to Animal Welfare at the Levels of the European Economic Community and the Council of Europe*, Eurogroup for Animal Welfare, Brussels

Humane Society International (1999) *Evolving: Moving into the New Millennium – How Customary International Law can Change the IWC*, Opening Statement of the 51st Meeting of the International Whaling Commission, Grenada, May 1999, Humane Society International, Washington

MAFF (1996) *Summary of the Law Relating to Farm Animal Welfare*, PB2531, MAFF, London

Michell, A R and Ewbank, R (eds) (1998) *Ethics, Welfare, Law and Market Forces: The Veterinary Interface*, Proceedings of RCVS and UFAW Symposium held at the RCVS, Nov 1996, UFAW, Wheathampstead

Parliamentary Education Unit (1997) *Making a Law*, Education Sheet 4, HMSO, London

RSPCA (1992) *Major Areas of Concern for Animal Welfare*, RSPCA Analysis, RSPCA, Horsham

WSPA (1999) *Focus on Legislation*, WSPA, Born Free Foundation, London/Dorking

Index